cute and easy

baby knits

25 adorable projects for 0–3 year olds

D0701843

Susie Johns

CICO BOOKS
LONDON NEW YORK

Dedication

To my babies: Josh, Lillie, and Edith.

Published in 2010 by CICO Books
An imprint of Ryland Peters & Small Ltd
20–21 Jockey's Fields   519 Broadway, 5th Floor
London WC1R 4BW   New York, NY 10012

www.cicobooks.com

10 9 8 7 6 5 4 3 2 1

A CIP catalog record for this book is available from the Library of Congress and the British Library.

ISBN: 978 1 907030 65 9

Printed in China

Editor: Kate Haxell
Designer: Christine Wood
Photographer: Emma Mitchell
Illustrators: Stephen Dew and Kate Simunek
Pattern checker: Marilyn Wilson
Stylist: Sania Pell

Acknowledgments

Thanks to Rowan, Coats Patons, Sirdar, and Designer Yarns (Debbie Bliss) for supplying the yarns used throughout this book. A big "thank you" to Cindy Richards and Sally Powell for asking me to do this book in the first place, to Pete Jorgensen for managing the project, to Kate for her invaluable editing skills, to Marilyn for her meticulous pattern-checking, to Emma for the stylish photography, and to Christine for the elegant page design. I should also like to thank the delightful models, as well as my little friends Katie, Anna, and Scarlet for helping during the design and development stages. Thanks to Nicky for knitting the ribbed vest and Patricia Liddle for knitting the hooded jacket, bloomers, and dungarees. Finally, a long-lasting "thank you" to my children for their patience and support.

contents

Introduction

What better way to celebrate the birth of a new baby than by knitting something special? Hand-crafted items, made with love, will not only show how much you care but will also keep the new arrival snug and warm. They may even be handed down to future generations—and every knitter knows that making little clothes and accessories is a real pleasure.

The knitting revival is in full swing and there has never been such a wide array of yarns available. I was taught to knit by my mother and grandmothers, but if you are from a different generation you may well have slipped through the knitting net, not knowing how to cast on or make a stitch, let alone how to follow a pattern. The good news is that you'll find a wealth of basic knitting know-how spread over the next few pages, and the projects in this book have been designed with the novice knitter in mind, so they should be easy enough for anyone to attempt.

Why not try one of the easiest and quickest patterns first, then move on to something a bit more challenging once you have gained some confidence? You could start with the Chunky Hat (see page 68) or, if you prefer something with slightly finer yarn and smaller needles, the Square-neck Sweater (see page 76). Then you could try making a pair of Soft Shoes (see page 70), as these are small and so quick to do, and will give you some practice in reading pattern instructions.

Of course, simple patterns like these are not just intended for the new knitter: many more experienced knitters will welcome a new batch of quick and easy patterns to create a whole layette—the traditional term for a complete set of clothing for a new baby—in next to no time.

Personal preferences

If you are new to knitting, you will soon find that you prefer certain methods, types of yarn, and sizes of needles to others. More seasoned knitters will also have their preferences.

For example, many of the projects for newborn babies—such as the Lacy Bootees, Lacy Mittens, and Traditional Bonnet (see pages 62–67), and the Wrapover Vest and Ribbed Vest (see pages 28–33)—are made with very fine yarn and thin needles. However, don't be put off by this because these projects are as quick, if not quicker, to make than chunkier items. Personally, I tend to favor finer yarns and needles as I find them easier to work with.

I also like working with color, particularly with Fair Isle designs, and you will find a few projects that feature colored borders or motifs, such as the Daisy Skirt (see page 56) and the little Heartwarmer top (see page 24). If you find the idea of using color too daunting, you can omit these details and work the appropriate number of rows in a plain color instead, or perhaps take an easier option of working a few colored stripes.

About the projects

Even before the baby arrives you can pick up needles and yarn to create a soft blanket or some bootees and mittens to fit the tiniest feet and hands, or maybe a huggable bear—the perfect baby gift.

I make no apologies for the fact that many of the items in this book, especially the ones for newborn babies, are very traditional. After all, these little garments are tried and tested and have been keeping small bodies warm for generations. I knitted classic vests, both pull-on and wrapover versions, for my own three babies and they are an excellent way to insulate against the cold. A new baby will spend most of the time asleep and simple items will keep your baby cozy and comfortable: a traditional vest in pure, soft wool (see page 28), a warm blanket (see page 104), or a snug all-in-one with a drawstring at the bottom (see page 108).

For outings, a bonnet or hat is a must to keep a baby's head warm, and perhaps a little cardigan or sweater as an extra layer. A pair of leggings complete with feet (see page 52) are perfect for all-over coziness.

Whatever your baby's birth weight, he or she will grow very rapidly and will quickly outgrow clothing—which is a good excuse to keep knitting. As your baby starts to crawl and explore his or her surroundings, different clothing is required, so projects include dungarees and a footless version of the leggings, as well as various tops. Then, when your baby becomes a toddler, there are sturdier items, including sweaters, cardigans, and a skirt and smock for girls, pretty enough for a party.

Yarns and needles

The essential equipment is a pair of knitting needles—though many people, including myself, prefer to use circular needles not only for knitting in the round but for knitting back and forth in rows. They can be less tiring on the hands and wrists, particularly if there are a large number of stitches, as the weight of the knitted fabric is distributed more evenly. And as the two ends are joined together, it is impossible for one of the needles to go missing.

Straight knitting needles are available in wood, plastic, aluminum, and bamboo, and you will discover through practice which suits you—and your knitting project—best. The key to choosing a good pair of knitting needles is that they should be smooth with well-shaped points. If you have the opportunity, try before you buy. Knitting departments in large stores may not offer this option but a specialist knitting shop will not only have sample needles for you to test but, usually, someone with knitting knowledge ready to offer advice. I like aluminum needles best, but many people swear by bamboo.

None of the projects in this book requires you to use sets of double-pointed needles to knit in the round, though the dress and skirt are both knitted in the round in one piece—using circular needles—which is really easy to do. However, you will need two double-pointed needles to knit cords for fastening the Candy-striped Cardigan (see page 34) and making the drawstring for the bottom of the Sleeping Robe (see page 108).

Other equipment needed includes stitch holders, which are like large safety pins, and a blunt tapestry needle for sewing garment pieces together and weaving in yarn ends. You will also need glass-headed pins for marking out gauge (tension) swatches and a ruler or tape measure for measuring gauge. Scissors will be necessary for snipping off yarn ends. Optional extras include stitch markers, which are small, open-ended plastic rings; you can improvise with a knotted loop of yarn. A row counter will help you keep track of how many rows you have knitted and rubber point protectors can be slipped on to needle points to prevent your work from falling off the needles.

The yarns used have been carefully selected. You will see that, for newborn babies, fine, pure wool yarns—both three-ply and four-ply—have been used because these are not only gentle on the skin but they also have good insulating properties. Where double-knitting weight yarns have been used, most contain blends with a high content of soft, natural fibers such as cashmere, wool, and silk. I do not hesitate to recommend what may seem to to be luxury yarns as I would want the best for my baby and these tiny garments take such a relatively small amount of yarn that the cost shouldn't be prohibitive. Natural yarns are these days often machine-washable on a gentle cycle, making them practical as well as pretty.

However, if you are knitting on a budget, go ahead and make substitutions for the recommended yarns. Just make sure you knit a gauge (tension) swatch before you begin—so that you can make the necessary adjustments with regards to needle sizes—and allow for the fact that you may need more or less yarn than the amounts given.

Now that I have passed on all the advice I can think of, it's time to select a project and start knitting. I loved knitting little clothes for my babies and it gives me a very warm feeling when I consider that a new generation of babies will be wearing garments made from the patterns I have created for this book.

Susie Johns

- holding needles and yarn • casting on • knit and purl
- binding (casting) off • shaping • sewing up
- understanding patterns • embroidery • following a chart
- color knitting

chapter one

knitting know-how

Learning to knit

The magic of knitting is the realization of just how simple it is to create a soft, supple fabric from a ball of yarn and some knitting needles. In this section you will find explanations and illustrations of the techniques used to make the knitted garments and accessories in this book.

Master the basics—casting on, forming knit and purl stitches, and binding (casting) off—and you are ready to get going on the simpler projects. Add to these basic skills by learning to shape pieces of knitting (by increasing and decreasing) and to work with texture and color (not as difficult as it may seem), then learn how to stitch pieces together and you can make any of the projects in this book.

Holding needles and yarn

If you are a knitting novice, you will need to discover which is the most comfortable way for you to hold your needles. This applies when using either a pair of knitting needles or a circular needle.

Like a knife

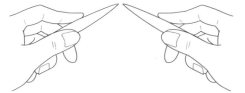

Pick up the needles, one in each hand, as if you were holding a knife and fork—that is to say, with your hands lightly over the top of each needle. As you knit, you will tuck the blunt end of the right-hand needle under your arm, let go with your hand and use your hand to manipulate the yarn, returning your hand to the needle to move the stitches along.

Like a pen

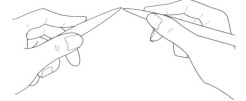

Now try changing the right hand so you are holding the needle as you would hold a pen, with your thumb and forefinger lightly gripping the needle close to its pointed tip and the shaft resting in the crook of your thumb. As you knit, you will not need to let go of the needle but simply slide your right hand forward to manipulate the yarn.

Holding the yarn

As you knit, you will be working stitches off the left needle and on to the right needle, and the yarn you are working with needs to be tensioned and manipulated to produce an even fabric. To hold and tension the yarn you can use either your right or left hand. Try both methods to discover which works best for you.

Yarn in right hand

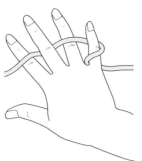

With the ball of yarn on the right, catch the yarn around your little finger then lace it over the third finger, under the middle finger and over the first finger of your right hand.

Yarn in left hand

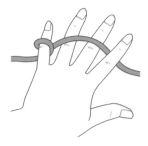

With the ball of yarn on your left, catch the yarn around your little finger then take it over the third and middle fingers. Most left-handed knitters will also find that, even if they reverse the direction of knitting (working stitches off the right needle onto the left needle), using the left hand to manipulate the yarn will be easier to manage.

Making a slip knot

Before you knit your first stitch, you will need to make a loop in the yarn. Follow these two simple steps.

With the ball of yarn to your right and the yarn end to the left, wrap a loop of yarn loosely around the first two fingers of your left hand, crossing over once. Holding a knitting needle in your right hand, insert the tip under the lower strand, as shown in the diagram, and pull it through to form a loop at the front.

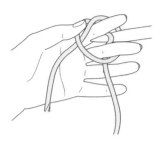

Slip the yarn off your fingers, leaving the loop on the needle. Gently pull the yarn end on the left to tighten the knot and the length of yarn on the right, leading to the ball of yarn, to tighten the loop on the needle.

Casting on

This technique, sometimes called the thumb method, is usually considered to be the easiest and most versatile way of casting on.

1. Leave a long end, about ³⁄₄in (2cm) per stitch to be cast on, before making a slip knot; the slip knot counts as the first stitch. Holding the needle and the yarn leading to the ball in your right hand, use the free end of yarn to make a loop around your left thumb. As you do this, tension the yarn between the third and fourth fingers of your left hand. Insert the needle tip into the loop.

2. Bring the yarn leading to the ball up between your thumb and the needle then take it around the needle, as shown in the illustration.

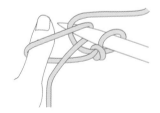

3. Draw the yarn through to make a stitch on the needle, then release the loop from the left thumb and gently pull on the yarn end to tension (tighten) the stitch.

Knit and purl

Now you need to learn to do some knitting. Here are the basic principles of forming a knit stitch and a purl stitch, the two fundamental stitches in all forms of knitting.

Making a knit stitch

Begin by holding the needle with the cast-on stitches in your left hand and the other needle in your right hand. The yarn from the ball should be hanging at the back of the work. You will be working into each stitch on the left needle in turn to complete a knit row.

1. Insert the right needle from left to right (knitwise) into the front of the first stitch. Take the yarn to the left, then up and around the tip of the right needle.

2. With the tip of the right needle, draw the yarn that is looped around that needle through the stitch on the left needle.

3. Drop the original stitch off the left needle to make a new knit stitch on the right needle.

Making a purl stitch

Hold the needles as you would when making a knit stitch, but with the yarn from the ball hanging at the front of the work. Work into each stitch on the left needle in turn to complete a purl row. The method given below assumes that you are holding the yarn in your right hand. If you hold it in your left hand, be sure to take it over the needle before pulling it through; wrapping it under the needle may seem an easier action to perform but it will result in your stitches facing the wrong way.

1. Insert the right needle from right to left (purlwise) into the front of the first stitch. Take the yarn over and around the tip of the right needle.

2. Dip the tip of the right needle and draw the yarn that is looped around that needle through the stitch on the left needle.

3. Drop the original stitch off the left needle to make a new purl stitch on the right needle.

Binding (casting) off

Although there are various methods used to bind (cast) off stitches, this is the most common and the easiest to perfect. When you work every stitch as a knit stitch, it will produce an edge that looks like a chain. In some patterns, the instructions are given to "bind (cast) off in rib", in which case you will need to knit the knit stitches and purl the purl stitches as you bind (cast) off, creating a softer, stretchier edge.

1. Work the first two stitches of the bind-off (cast-off) row then use the point of the left needle to lift the first stitch over the second stitch and off the right needle. Then work the next stitch so there are, once again, two stitches on the right needle and repeat the process, lifting one stitch over the other and off the needle. Continue until there is only one stitch remaining on the right needle.

2. Break the yarn, leaving a tail of yarn long enough for sewing any seams. Draw the end of the yarn through the remaining stitch, slip it off the needle and pull tightly to secure.

Shaping

By working increases and decreases, you can shape pieces of knitting to make a garment.
Some of these techniques can also be used to create various stitch patterns.

Increasing

Each of the methods described here produces a different effect. For example, knitting into the front and back of a stitch creates a bar at the base of the new stitch; the lifted strand is almost invisible; while the yarnover creates a hole, which can be used for lacy patterns or to create a buttonhole.

Knit into the front and back

When you see the abbreviation "inc 1", you will need to begin by knitting the stitch in the usual way. However, before dropping it from the left needle, take the right needle tip behind the left needle and knit into the stitch again, but this time into the back of it. Then drop the original stitch off the left needle, leaving the two new stitches on the right needle.

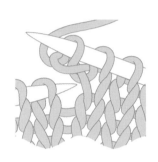

Make one stitch

The abbreviation for this is "M1". Bring the left needle forward and, inserting the tip from front to back, lift up the horizontal strand that lies between the two needles. Take the right needle behind the left needle to knit into the back of the strand.

Yarnover

When you see the instruction "yo", it means you either have to bring the yarn to the front of the work or take it to the back, depending on the stitch combination you are working on.

Between two knit stitches, bring the yarn between the needles to the front of the work, put the tip of the right needle into the next stitch on the left needle, then take the yarn over the right needle to the back, ready to knit the stitch (as shown in the illustration).

Between a knit and a purl stitch, bring the yarn to the front, over the needle, and back to the front again before putting the tip of the right needle into the next stitch to purl it.

Between two purl stitches, take the yarn over and right around the needle and to the front again before the tip of the right needle and into the next stitch to purl it.

Between a purl and a knit stitch, put the tip of the right needle into the next stitch on the left needle, take the yarn over the right needle and to the back to knit the stitch.

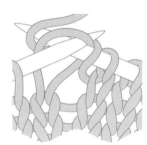

In each case, the action of taking the yarn over the needle will create an additional stitch on that needle.

Decreasing

It is important to employ the various methods described here in the correct place, as the decreases cause stitches to slant either to the right or the left; the instructions for each project will give guidance as to which method to use. For example, knitting two stitches together (abbreviated to "k2tog") creates a decrease that slants to the right, while passing a slipped stitch over a knitted stitch ("skpo") creates a slant to the left. These slanted stitches are used to decorative effect in the raglan sleeve shaping on the Fish Sweater (see page 88) and on sloped front openings, such as for the Wrapover Vest (see page 28).

Knitting stitches together

When you see the abbreviation "k2tog", insert the right needle knitwise through the fronts of the first two stitches on the left needle, then knit them together in the same way as you would knit a single stitch and slip both stitches off the left needle, leaving one stitch on the right needle. The second stitch lies on top and the decrease slants to the right.

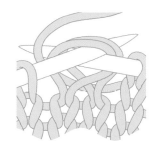

Pass slipped stitch over

For the abbreviation "skpo", you will need to slip the first stitch knitwise, knit the next stitch, then use the tip of the left needle to lift the slipped stitch over the knitted one and off the right needle. The first stitch lies on top and the decrease slants to the left.

Two-stitch decrease 1

Used for lacy stitch patterns as well as for shaping, this method involves slipping the first stitch knitwise, knitting the next two stitches together, then lifting the slipped stitch over and off the right needle. The slipped stitch lies on top and slants to the left, while the knitted stitches underneath slant to the right. This decrease is abbreviated to "sk2po".

Two-stitch decrease 2

This decrease is also used both for shaping and for stitch patterns. Insert the tip of the right needle through the fronts of the first two stitches on the left needle as if to knit two together, but slip these stitches, unworked, on to the right needle. Knit the next stitch, then use the tip of the left needle to lift the two slipped stitches over and off the right needle. The center stitch lies on top and the two side stitches slope toward it. This decrease is written out as "sl2, k1, psso".

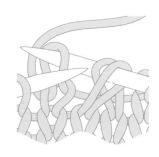

Picking up stitches

Sometimes the edges of a garment—such as the neckband of a sweater or the button bands on the front of a jacket or cardigan—are created by picking up stitches along the row ends. For a neat finish, be consistent as to where you insert the needle in the knitted fabric.

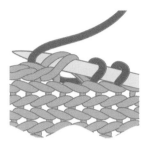

To make the first stitch, working from right to left, insert the tip of the needle between the edge stitch and the next stitch in from the edge of the knitted fabric, take the yarn around the needle and pull the loop through to make a stitch. Continue in this way along the row ends, always working one stitch in from the edge, until you have the required number of stitches on the needle.

If you need to pick up fewer stitches than there are row ends, use pins to mark sections along the edge, then divide the number of stitches you need to pick up by the number of sections. Pick up the same number of stitches from each section to ensure that your stitches are spaced evenly.

Sewing up

When you have taken time and trouble to knit the various pieces of a garment, it is important to take as much time and trouble to join them together. Badly stitched seams can completely spoil the appearance of a knitted garment—but if you follow the methods shown here, you will be able to create a really neat, professional finish.

Before stitching seams, check the ball band of the yarn you have used for pressing instructions. If the pieces need to be pressed (the pattern will tell you), do this before you start sewing them up.

Mattress stitch on row ends

This is used to join the edges of two pieces of knitted fabric to create a virtually invisible seam, perfect for the side seams on a sweater.

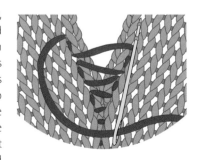

Place the two pieces, right sides up, with the side edges matching. Thread a blunt-tipped tapestry needle with matching yarn (a contrast color is used here to help you see what's happening), and attach the yarn to the bottom corner of one of the pieces, on the wrong side. Bring the needle through to the front of that piece, between the edge stitch and

the second stitch in the first row. Insert the tip of the needle between the edge stitch and the second stitch on the other piece, then pass the needle upward, under the loops of one or two rows and back through to the front. Insert the needle into the same hole where the last stitch emerged on the opposite piece and pass it upward, under the loops of one or two rows and back through to the front. Repeat this process, zigzagging from one side to the other and always taking the needle under the same number of loops (either one loop for chunky knits or two for finer knits), taking care not to miss any rows. After every few stitches, pull up the yarn to close the two sides together, but do not pull too tightly or you will distort or pucker the seam.

Mattress stitch on cast on and bound (cast) off edges

This is worked in a similar way to mattress stitch on row ends.

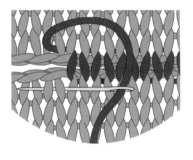

Place the two pieces, right sides up, with the edges to be joined touching. Thread a needle and attach the yarn to the wrong side of one piece. Bring the needle through to the front of that piece, between the first stitch and the second stitch in the first row. Insert the tip of the needle between the first stitch and the second stitch on the other piece, then pass the needle under both strands of the second stitch and back through to the front. Insert the needle into the same hole where the last stitch emerged on the opposite piece and pass it under both strands of the second stitch and back through to the front. Repeat this process, zigzagging from one side to the other and always taking the needle under both strands of the next stitch along. Pull up the yarn to close the seam.

Troubleshooting

One of the things beginners most fear is dropping a stitch—but if this happens, it should not be a cause for panic. Use a safety pin or small stitch holder to capture the dropped stitch and hold it in place while you remedy the situation. If the dropped stitch is on the row you are currently working on, slip the stitches you have already worked back on to the left needle until you reach the dropped stitch, pick up the dropped stitch with the tips of the knitting needles, then slip the worked stitches back on to the right needle until you are back on track.

If the dropped stitch is below the row you are currently working on, slip stitches until you are above it, then use a crochet hook to pick it up.

Picking up a dropped stitch in the same row

Insert the right needle into the dropped stitch, then under the strand between neighboring stitches on the row above. Use the left needle to lift the dropped stitch over the strand and off the right needle, then slip the stitch, if necessary, so that it faces in the right direction (the same direction as all the other stitches on the needle).

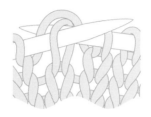

Picking up a dropped stitch from a previous row

A dropped stitch further down the work will create a ladder. Insert a crochet hook into the dropped stitch at the base of the ladder, then catch the strand lying between the stitches on the row immediately above and pull it through the dropped stitch. Continue in this way until all the strands have been turned back into stitches, then transfer the last stitch on to the left needle.

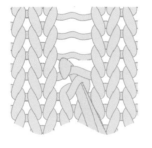

Simple knitted fabrics

Knit and purl stitches can be combined to create a number of attractive stitch patterns. The ones shown on this page appear in patterns in this book, and they are easy to memorize. More complex decorative combinations of knit and purl stitches are used to good effect in the Cardigan with Frill (see page 38) and the Fisherman's Sweater (see page 80), where charts are provided to show the positions of the knit and purl stitches in each row.

Garter stitch

To make this fabric you just knit every row. The resulting fabric has clearly defined horizontal ridges.

Stockinette (stocking) stitch

This fabric consists of alternate knit and purl rows. The smooth side of each stitch is on one side of the fabric and the looped side of each stitch is on the other, giving a recognizable "right" and "wrong" side to the fabric. The smooth (right) side is called stockinette (stocking) stitch and the ridged (wrong) side is referred to as "reverse stockinette (stocking) stitch".

stockinette (stocking) stitch

reverse stockinette
(stocking) stitch

Rib

For single rib (as shown), alternate stitches along a row are knitted and purled. On the following row, the knit stitches are purled and the purl stitches are knitted, resulting in a fabric with distinct vertical rows of stitches and good elasticity.

Seed (moss) stitch

As with single rib, alternate stitches along a row are knitted and purled—but on the following row, the knit stitches are knitted and the purl stitches purled, so instead of stitches lining up to form vertical rows, a textured, reversible fabric is created.

Understanding patterns

To save space, knitting instructions are abbreviated. At first glance, especially to the uninitiated, this strange code may look impenetrable. However, once you understand the basic principles of reading a pattern, a whole new world of knitting possibilities will open up to you.

But even when you have deciphered the language of the pattern—k1, sl1, p1, psso, and so on—and are eager to begin work on your project, there are a few things you need to consider.

Sizes

Some patterns will be for one size only, while some garments are offered in a range of sizes. Where the pattern is for more than one size, the smallest size is given first, followed by larger sizes within brackets and separated by colons. These brackets will also appear throughout the pattern and, once you have selected the size you wish to make, it is important that you follow the instructions that relate to this size.

To help you choose which size to make, the dimensions of the finished project are given.

Gauge (tension)

In order for your knitted project to be the right size, you need to make sure you are working to the gauge (tension) given in the pattern instructions. The gauge is the number of stitches and rows produced over a given measurement, which is usually 4in (10cm).

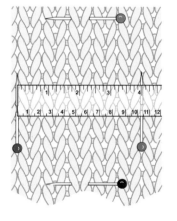

Using the recommended needles and yarn, knit a swatch (a small piece of knitted fabric), casting on a few more stitches than the number given in the gauge instruction, and knitting a few more rows, too. Count and mark off with pins the correct number of stitches and rows, then measure this area using a ruler or tape measure.

If your marked area of stitches and rows measures less than 10cm (4in), your knitting is tighter than the gauge required for this pattern and you will need to knit another swatch using larger needles. If it measures more than 10cm (4in), your knitting is looser than required for the pattern, and you will need to try again with smaller needles.

This may sound time-consuming, but it is quicker than knitting the whole project and then having to re-knit it because it came out the wrong size.

Materials and tools

The knitting needles and yarn, and any other items you will need to complete the project, are listed at the beginning of the pattern instructions. Once you have knitted and measured your gauge (tension) swatch, you may, of course, need to use different-sized needles from the ones specified.

If you choose to use a yarn other than the one recommended, you may need more or less yarn than the amount given and you must knit a swatch to make sure that the substitute yarn will knit to the same gauge (tension).

It's the length of yarn in a ball, not the weight of the ball, that's important if you do substitute a yarn. Each pattern tells you the number of balls needed and the total length of yarn in yards and meters. Check the ball band of the substitute yarn to see how much it contains, then multiply that by the number of balls needed to see if the same number of balls provides you with enough yarn.

Abbreviations

There are some standard abbreviations that apply to most patterns. If a pattern includes any special instructions, your attention will be drawn to this.

Most abbreviations are easy to remember—such as "k" for knit and "p" for purl—while others appear to be more cryptic until you understand what they mean. A few—such as "sk2po" for "slip 1 stitch, knit 2 stitches together, pass slipped stitch over"—refer to not one action but a series of related actions.

Square brackets are used to denote how many times an action or series of actions needs to be repeated.

Asterisks indicate where to begin and end a series of actions, which are often repeated elsewhere in the pattern.

beg	begin(ning)
cont	continue
dec	decrease
foll	following
inc 1	knit into front and back of stitch
k	knit
k2tog	knit 2 stitches together
p	purl
patt	pattern
psso	pass slipped stitch(es) over
RS	right side
skpo	slip 1 stitch, knit 1 stitch, pass slipped stitch over
sk2po	slip 1 stitch, knit 2 stitches together, pass slipped stitch over
sl	slip
sl st	slip stitch
st st	stockinette (stocking) stitch
WS	wrong side
[ ]	work instructions within square brackets as directed

Yarn information

Debbie Bliss Cotton DK; 100% cotton; approximately 91yds (84m) in a 1³/₄oz (50g) ball.

Debbie Bliss Donegal Luxury Tweed Aran; 85% wool, 15% angora; approximately 96yds (88m) in a 1³/₄oz (50g) ball.

Patons Fairytale Dreamtime 3ply; 100% pure wool; approximately 372yds (340m) in a 1³/₄oz (50g) ball.

Patons Wool Blend Aran; 63% wool, 37% acrylic; approximately 202yds (185m) in a 3¹/₂oz (100g) ball.

Regia Silk 4-ply; 55% new wool, 25% polyamide, 20% silk; approximately 230yds (210m) in a 1³/₄oz (50g) ball.

Regia Softy Color; 61% polyamide, 39% wool; approximately 137yds (125m) in a 1³/₄oz (50g) ball.

Rowan Baby Alpaca DK; 100% baby alpaca; approximately 109yds (100m) in a 1³/₄oz (50g) ball.

Rowan Cashsoft Baby DK; 57% extra fine merino wool, 33% acrylic microfiber, 10% cashmere; approximately 142yds (130m) in a 1³/₄oz (50g) ball.

Rowan Felted Tweed Chunky; 50% merino wool, 25% alpaca, 25% viscose; approximately 55yds (50m) in a 1³/₄oz (50g) ball.

Rowan Kid Classic; 70% lambswool, 26% kid mohair, 4% nylon; approximately 153yds (140m) in a 1³/₄oz (50g) ball.

Rowan Pure Wool DK; 100% superwash wool; approximately 137yds (125m) in a 1³/₄oz (50g) ball.

Rowan Scottish Tweed Aran; 100% wool; approximately 186yds (170m) in a 3¹/₂oz (100g) ball.

Rowan Silk Wool DK; 50% silk, 50% merino wool; approximately 109yds (100m) in a 1³/₄oz (50g) ball.

Rowan Wool Cotton; 50% wool, 50% cotton; approximately 123yds (113m) in a 1³/₄oz (50g) ball.

Sirdar Snuggly Baby Bamboo DK; 80% viscose (sourced from bamboo), 20% wool; approximately 104yds (95m) in a 1³/₄oz (50g) ball.

Sublime Baby Cashmere Merino Silk DK; 70% extra-fine merino wool; 20% silk, 5% cashmere; approximately 127yards (116 metres) in a 1³/₄oz (50g) ball.

Sublime Cashmere Merino Silk Aran; 70% extra-fine merino wool; 20% silk, 5% cashmere; approximately 94yds (86m) in a 1³/₄oz (50g) ball.

Sublime Luxurious Woolly Merino; 96% merino wool, 4% nylon; approximately 96yds (90m) in a 1³/₄oz (50g) ball.

Sublime Soya Cotton DK; 50% soya sourced viscose, 50% cotton; approximately 120yds (110m) in a 1³/₄oz (50g) ball.

Following a chart

A chart is simply a diagram of stitches. In this book, charts are used to show textured patterns created by working knit and purl stitches, and color patterns. Colored borders and motifs are a great way to add a touch of decorative detail to knitted garments. Geometric borders made up of pattern repeats are usually referred to as "Fair Isle", while motifs involving larger blocks of color and freeform shapes come under the heading of "intarsia". Instructions for working both techniques are on pages 20–21.

This collection of patterns includes some Fair Isle designs, such as the border of hearts on the Heartwarmer (see page 24) and the flowers on the hem of the Daisy Skirt (see page 57). There are also intarsia motifs, such as the goldfish on the Fish Sweater (see page 88).

In both Fair Isle and intarsia knitting, designs are provided on a chart, with a simple grid in which each colored square represents a stitch. Each chart has a key that tells you which yarn (A, B, C, etc in the materials list) is represented by which color square.

To work from a chart, read upward from the bottom line, and from right to left on knit rows, and left to right on purl rows. Unless otherwise stated, the first row (bottom row) of a chart is the first row of the color pattern and is usually a knit row. For a small area, you will be given a chart showing the whole design. For a repeated pattern there will be a chart showing the section of the design to be repeated and just a few of the repeats. Shown below is a sample chart with its key and the pattern repeat marked. The repeat is ten stitches and the paler-colored part of the chart shows you how the repeat works to form the design. This chart is actually the one for the Daisy Skirt (see page 58).

The loops of yarn formed at the back of the work are called "floats" and, if the gap between colors is less than four stitches, they can be stranded. If the gaps are four stitches or more, the floats should be woven in as you go (see page 20). When working colored patterns on baby knits, you should try to avoid having long floats on the inside of the garments, in case little fingers and toes get caught up when putting clothes on or taking them off.

With intarsia designs involving blocks of color, such as the fishes (see page 88), instead of working from a single ball of yarn, it is often easier to make up a separate small ball or skein of yarn for each motif. You will need to twist yarns together at the back of the work as you change colors, to avoid creating gaps between stitches (see page 20).

Whichever method you use—stranding, weaving, or color change—make sure the yarn is not pulled too tightly, or the work will become puckered and will not have the right amount of elasticity.

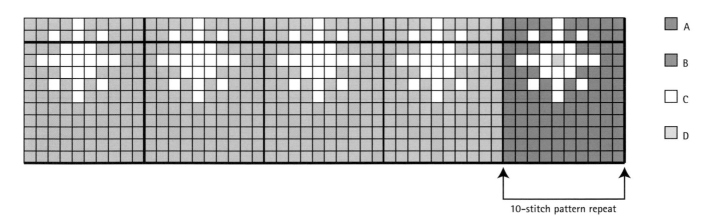

A
B
C
D

10-stitch pattern repeat

Color knitting

Shown here are the techniques for changing colors and weaving in floats. If you haven't done any color knitting before, practice the techniques with scrap yarn before embarking on a project.

Stranding

The different-colored yarns form short strands—or floats—across the back of the work.

1. On a knit row, try to hold the first color in your right hand and the second color in your left hand. If you find this too difficult, then simply hold the color that you are using and let the other color dangle until you need it. Knit the required number of stitches in the first color.

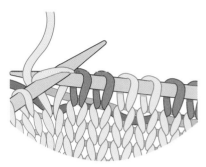

2. When you need to work stitches in the second color, if you are using both hands to hold the yarns simply insert the right needle into the stitch and draw a loop of yarn from your left hand through the stitch. Otherwise, drop the color you have been using and pick up the second color. Whichever method you use, allow the color not in use to form a strand, not too tight or too loose, across the back (wrong side) of the work.

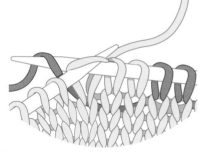

3. On a purl row, hold the yarns as for the knit rows. The colors not in use will form strands across the front (wrong side) of the work. Purl the required number of stitches in the first color. When it comes to purling a stitch in the second color, insert the right-hand needle into the next stitch and draw a loop through from the yarn

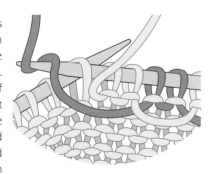

held in the left hand, as before, or drop the first color, allowing it to dangle, and pick up the second color if you find this method easier.

Weaving

The different-colored floats are caught in by the working yarn at the back of the work. You need to do this if there is an interval of more than four stitches between a color being used.

1. As you make a stitch, lay the yarn not in use over the point of the right-hand needle, then complete the stitch with the working yarn, taking care not to knit in the contrast yarn. The yarn not in use will have been woven in to the back of the work. Repeat this process on every third or fourth stitch.

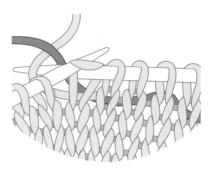

2. On purl rows, use the same method to weave in the yarn not in use, taking it across the working yarn on every third or fourth stitch. Do not weave the yarn in on every stitch or on every second stitch as this can distort the stitches and alter the gauge (tension) of the fabric.

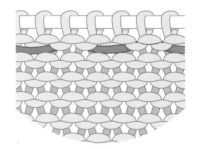

Color change (intarsia)

1. On a right-side row, with the yarns at the back of the work, where there is a diagonal color change with a slant to the right or a vertical color change, as you change colors take the first color over the second color, drop it, then pick up the second color underneath, thus crossing the strands of yarn over each other. If the different-colored yarns do not interlock in this way a gap will form between the stitches.

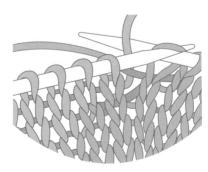

Embroidery

Embroidered motifs are a good way of adding a touch of detail and contrasting color to a knitted garment. Use the even pattern of horizontal and vertical rows of knitted stitches as a grid when working the motifs.

The Sleeping Robe (see page 108) has a simple embroidered design worked in satin stitch and lazy daisy stitch. Use yarn of a similar or lighter weight to that used for the knitting: if the yarn is too thick it can distort the fabric, and if it is too fine the embroidery tends to disappear between the knitted stitches.

Before you start to stitch, thread the yarn into a blunt-tipped tapestry needle and fasten the end of the yarn into the back of a few stitches on the wrong side of the knitted fabric.

Satin stitch

Bring the needle and yarn through to the right side of the knitted fabric and work parallel stitches, close together, across several knitted stitches in a row. Do not pull the yarn too tightly or it will pucker the fabric.

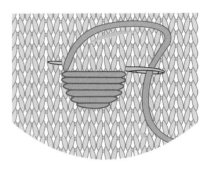

Lazy daisy

Bring the needle and yarn up through the knitted fabric where you want the base of the petal to be, then take it back down through the fabric in the same place, leaving a loop of yarn on the front. Bring the tip of the needle up through the fabric, through the loop of yarn and back down on the other side of the loop to secure it in place. Repeat for each petal.

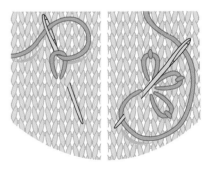

2. On a wrong-side row, with the yarns at the front of the work, when there is a diagonal color change with a slant to the left or a vertical color change, make sure you cross the first color over the second color before using the second color to form the next stitch, thus crossing the strands of yarn over each other.

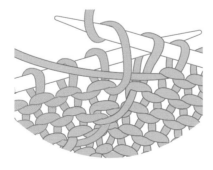

• heartwarmer • wrapover vest • ribbed vest
• candy-striped cardigan • cardigan with frill

chapter two

vests and cardigans

heartwarmer

This pretty crossover top provides an extra layer to wear over a T-shirt, dress, or rompers to keep baby's chest nice and warm. The border of hearts adds decorative detail and the matching cord tie is a delightful finishing touch.

Yarn
2(2:2) x 1¾oz (50g) balls—approx 254yds (232m)—of Sublime Baby Cashmere Merino Silk DK in shade 121 Mousse (A) and 1(1:1) ball—approx 127yds (116m)—in shade 102 Jammy (B)

Needles
Pair each of US 3 (3.25mm) and US 2 (2.75mm) knitting needles
2 US 2 (3.00mm) double-pointed knitting needles

Extras
Tapestry needle
1 x ½in (12mm) button
Sewing needle
Sewing thread to match yarn

Sizes
3(6:9) months

Actual size
Width across back: 9(10:11¼)in (23(25.5:28.5)cm)

Gauge (tension)
23 sts and 30 rows to 4in (10cm) over stockinette (stocking) stitch using US 3 (3.25mm) needles.

Abbreviations
See page 17.

Pattern

Back
With US 2 (2.75mm) needles and yarn A, cast on 52(58:64) sts.
Row 1: [P1, k1] to end.
Rep this row 7 times more.
Change to US 3 (3.25mm) needles.
Beg with a k row, work in stockinette (stocking) stitch (1 row knit, 1 row purl) for 4 rows.
Join in yarn B and work 5 rows of chart.
Cont in yarn A, work a further 3(7:11) rows in stockinette (stocking) stitch with no further shaping.

Shape armholes
Next row: Bind (cast) off 3 sts, k to end. *49(55:61) sts*
Next row: Bind (cast) off 3 sts, p to end. *46(52:58) sts*
Next row: Bind (cast) off 2 sts, k to end. *44(50:56) sts*
Next row: Bind (cast) off 2 sts, p to end. *42(48:54) sts*
Dec 1 st at beg of next 4(6:8) rows. *38(42:46) sts*
Cont in stockinette (stocking) stitch without further shaping until work measures 6¾(7½:8¼)in (17(19:21)cm) from cast-on edge, ending with a purl row.

Shape shoulder and neck
Row 1: Bind (cast) off 5(6:7) sts, then k 7(8:9) sts, turn and leave rem sts on a stitch holder.
Row 2: Bind (cast) off 3 sts, p to end. *5(6:7) sts*
Bind (cast) off rem sts.
Rejoin yarn to sts on holder.
Next row: Bind (cast) off 12(12:12) sts, k to end. *13(15:17) sts*
Next row: Bind (cast) off 5(6:7) sts, p to end. *8(9:10) sts*
Next row: Bind (cast) off 3 sts, k to end. *5(6:7) sts*
Bind (cast) off rem sts.

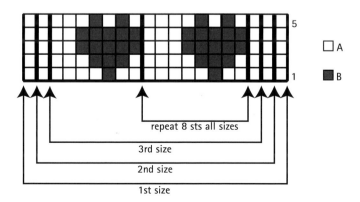

Knitting notes The chart shows you the 8-stitch pattern that you need to repeat to make the band of hearts. In addition the number of edge stitches needed at the begining and end of the band is marked for each size. So, if you are knitting, for example, the 1st size, on the first row (which is a knit row) work the first 3 sts as indicated from the right of the chart, then repeat the 8-stitch marked section until you reach the last 9 stitches on the left-hand needle, then work the last 9 stitches as indicated.

Right front

With US 2 (2.75mm) needles and yarn A, cast on 52(58:64) sts.
Row 1: [P1, k1] to end.
Rep this row 7 times more.
Change to US 3 (3.25mm) needles.
Beg with a k row, work in stockinette (stocking) stitch for 4 rows.
Join in yarn B and work 2 rows of chart.
Starting on 3rd row of chart, beg front shaping: bind (cast) off 2, k to end.
50(56:62) sts
Complete 4th row of chart, dec 1 at front edge. *49(55:61) sts*
On 5th row of chart, dec 1, k to end.
Cont in yarn A, work in stockinette (stocking) stitch dec 1 st on front edge on every row for a further 4(8:12) rows, ending with a knit row.

Shape armhole

Bind (cast) off 3 sts at beg of next row, 2 sts at beg of next alt row and 1 st on armhole edge of next 2(3:4) alt rows, at the same time, dec 1 st on front edge of every row until 10(12:14) sts rem.
Cont without further shaping until Front matches Back to beg of shoulder shaping, ending at armhole edge.

Shape shoulder

Bind (cast) off 5(6:7) sts at beg of next row. *5(6:7) sts*
Work 1 row.
Bind (cast) off rem sts.

Left front

Work as for Right Front, but reversing shaping.

Borders

Armhole bands

Stitch shoulder seams.
With right side facing, using US 2 (2.75mm) needles and yarn A, pick up and knit 73(79:85) sts around armhole edge.
Row 1: K1, [p1, k1] to end.
Row 2: P1, [k1, p1] to end.
Rep row 1 once more.
Bind (cast) off in rib.
Rep for second armhole.

Front borders and neck

Stitch side seams.
Fold ribbing on lower edge in half to wrong side and slip stitch cast-on edge to last row of ribbing.
With right side facing, using US 2 (2.75mm) needles and yarn A, and starting on 2nd st up from folded edge, pick up and knit 7 sts up straight edge on right front, 55(61:67) sts up right front sloping edge to shoulder, 22(24:26) sts across back neck, 55(61:67) sts down left front sloping edge, and 8 sts down straight edge on left front. *147(161:175) sts*

Row 1: K1, [p1, k1] to end.
Row 2: P1, [k1, p1] to end.
Rep row 1 once more.
Bind (cast) off in rib.

Cord tie

With US 2 (3.00mm) double-pointed needles, cast on 3 sts.
Row 1: K3, do not turn but slide sts to other end of needle. Rep row 1, pulling yarn tightly across back of work, until work measures 17¾in (45cm).
Bind (cast) off.
Stitch center of cord in place on outside, at base of left side seam.

To finish

Weave in any loose ends neatly.
On corner of left front make a buttonhole loop in matching yarn. Stitch a button on inside, at base of right side seam, to correspond with button loop.

wrapover vest

The ideal gift for a newborn baby, this snug, short-sleeved vest is too pretty to hide under other clothes. The silk yarn is both soft against delicate skin and deliciously warm to wear.

Knitting notes The garment pieces are worked from the shoulder down to the hem and the sleeves are worked from top to bottom. On the two front pieces, the border is formed as you go, making it easy and quick. If you want to avoid stitching the sleeves in place, instead of making them separately you may wish to join the shoulder seams then pick up and knit the stitches on the armhole edge, reducing the amount of sewing-up. Similarly, instead of working the ribbed hem on the back and each of the two front pieces, you may prefer to leave it unworked, stitch the side seams, then pick up and knit 134 stitches along the lower edge.

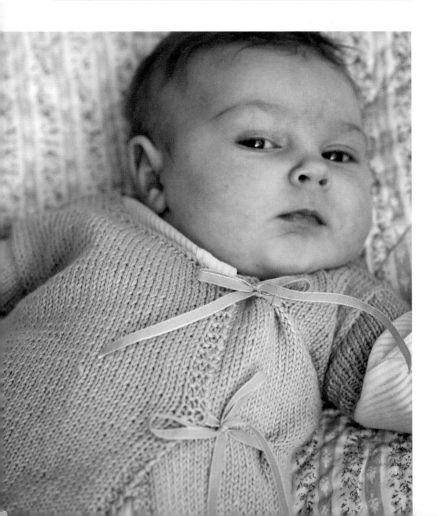

Yarn
2 x 1¾oz (50g) balls—approx 460yds (420m)—of Regia Silk 4 ply in shade 54 blue-grey

Needles
Pair each of US 2 (3.00mm) and US 1 (2.25mm) knitting needles

Extras
Tapestry needle
31½in (80cm) of ¼-in (6-mm) wide ribbon
Sewing needle
Sewing thread to match yarn

Sizes
Newborn

Actual size
Width across back: 8½in (21.5cm)
Shoulder to hem: 9in (23cm)

Gauge (tension)
26 sts and 40 rows to 4in (10cm) over stockinette (stocking) stitch using US 2 (3.00mm) needles.

Abbreviations
See page 17.

Pattern

Back
With US 2 (3.00mm) needles, beg at back neck edge, cast on 56 sts.
Beg with a k row, work in stockinette (stocking) stitch (1 row knit, 1 row purl) for 86 rows.
Change to US 1 (2.25mm) needles.
Row 87: [K1, p1] to end.
Rep row 87, 3 times more
Bind (cast) off in rib.

Right front
With US 2 (3.00mm) needles, cast on 19 sts for shoulder.
Row 1: Knit.
Row 2: Sl1, k2, purl to end.
Rep rows 1–2, 4 times more.
Row 11: K to last 4 sts, inc 1, k3.
Row 12: Sl1, k1, inc 1, p to end.
Rows 13–32: Rep rows 11–12, 10 times more. *41 sts*
Rows 33–86: Rep rows 1–2 27 times.
Change to US 1 (2.25mm) needles.
Next row: K1, [p1, k1] to end.
Next row: P1, [k1, p1] to end.
Rep last 2 rows once more.
Bind (cast) off in rib.

Left front

With US 2 (3.00mm) needles, cast on 19 sts for shoulder.
Row 1: Sl 1, knit to end.
Row 2: Purl to last 3 sts, k3.
Rep rows 1–2, 4 times more.
Row 11: Sl1, k1, inc 1, k to end.
Row 12: Purl to last 4 sts, inc 1, k3.
Rows 13–32: Rep rows 11–12, 10 times more. *41 sts*
Rows 33–86: Rep rows 1–2 27 times.
Change to US 1 (2.25mm) needles
Next row: K1, [p1, k1] to end.
Next row: P1, [k1, p1] to end.
Rep last 2 rows once more.
Bind (cast) off in rib.

Sleeves (make two)

With US 2 (3.00mm) needles, cast on 45 sts.
Beg with a k row, work in stockinette (stocking) stitch for 4 rows.
Change to US 1 (2.25mm) needles.
Row 5: K1, skpo, k to last 3 sts, k2tog, k1. *43 sts*
Beg with a purl row, work in stockinette (stocking) stitch for 3 rows.
Row 9: K1, skpo, k to last 3 sts, k2tog, k1. *41 sts*
Row 10: Purl.
Row 11: K1, [p1, k1] to end.
Row 12: P1, [k1, p1] to end.
Rep rows 11–12 once more.
Bind (cast) off in rib.

To finish

Weave in any loose ends neatly.
Join shoulder seams. Matching center of cast-on edge of sleeve to shoulder seam, attach sleeves. Stitch side and sleeve seams.
Cut four lengths of ribbon, each measuring 8in (20.5cm). Stitch two pieces to the front edge of the right front for girls, or the left front for boys, and the other two pieces to the opposite side (see photo of finished vest for guidance).

ribbed vest

This top will keep baby cozy and comfortable whatever the weather. Fine yarn is perfect for a small baby, creating a thin but very warm layer next to the skin.

Yarn
1(1:2) x 1³/₄oz (50g) balls—approx 339(339:678)yds (310m(310:620)m)—of Patons Fairytale Dreamtime 3 ply in shade 2931 Ivory

Needles
Pair each of US 2 (2.75mm) and US 1 (2.25mm) knitting needles

Extras
Tapestry needle
19³/₄in (50cm) of ⅛-in (3-mm) wide ribbon in each of two colors

Sizes
0-3(3-6:6-9)months

Actual size
Around chest: 14¼(16¼:18)in (36(41:46)cm) when stretched slightly

Gauge (tension)
28 sts and 42 rows to 4in (10cm) over stockinette (stocking) stitch, using US 2 (2.75mm) needles.

Abbreviations
See page 17.

Pattern
Back
With US 2 (2.75mm) needles, cast on 68(77:86) sts.
Row 1: (RS): K2, [p1, k2] to end.
Row 2: P2, [k1, p2] to end.
Rep rows 1-2 until work measures 8³/₄(9½:10¼)in (22(24:26)cm) from cast-on edge, ending with a WS row.
Shape shoulders
Bind (cast) off 16(19:23) sts at the beginning of the next 2 rows, leave the rem 36(39:40) sts on a stitch holder.

Front
Follow instructions for Back until work measures 6(6³/₄:7½)in (15(17:19)cm) from cast-on edge, ending with a WS row.
Shape neck
Next row: Continuing in rib patt, work 21(24:28) sts for Left Front and turn, leaving the rem sts on a stitch holder.
Left front
Next row: Dec 1, patt to end.

Next row: Patt to end. Rep last 2 rows until 16(19:23) sts rem.
Cont in rib patt, with no further shaping, until work measures 8³/₄(9½:10¼)in (22(24:26)cm) from cast-on edge.
Bind (cast) off.
Right front
Slip the center 26(29:30) sts on to a stitch holder, rejoin yarn to rem sts and complete
Right Front to match Left Front, but reversing shaping.

Neckband
Join right shoulder seam using backstitch. With right side of work facing and using US 1 (2.25 mm) needles, pick up and knit 19(20:23) sts down left front neck, then (working across stitches on holder) k2tog, k 22(25:26), k2tog, pick up and knit 19(20:23) sts up right front neck, then (working across stitches on holder) k2tog, k 32(35:36), k2tog. *96(104:112) sts*
Knit 1 row.
Next row (eyelets): K1, *yo, k2tog, k2, rep from * to last 3 sts, yo, k2tog, k1.
Knit 3 rows.
Bind (cast) off.

Armbands
Measure 5½(6:6¼)in (14(15:16)cm) up from the cast-on edge on Front and Back and place markers at each end of the row.
Left armband
Join left shoulder seam using backstitch.
With right side of work facing and starting and ending at markers, pick up and knit 60(68:76) sts evenly spaced around left armhole.
Knit 3 rows.
Bind (cast) off.
Right armband
Work as for Left Armband.

To finish
Weave in any loose ends neatly.
Join side seams.
Thread both pieces of ribbon through eyelets and tie ends in a bow.

candy-striped cardigan

With simple shaping, jaunty vertical stripes, and a tie-neck, this cardigan is both pretty and easy for baby to wear. The yarn is self-striping, so you don't even have to worry about changing colors.

Yarn
3(3:4) x 1¾oz (50g) balls—approx 411(411:548)yds (375(375:500)m)—of Regia Softy Color in shade 475 Baby Mix

Needles
Pair of US 5 (3.75mm) knitting needles
2 US 3 (3.25mm) double-pointed knitting needles

Extras
Tapestry needle

Sizes
6(9:12) months

Actual size
Across back: 10¾(11½:12¼)in (27(29:31)cm)
Shoulder to hem: 9(9½:10)in (23(24:25.5)cm)
Sleeve seam: 5(5½:6)in (13(14:15)cm)

Gauge (tension)
22 sts and 40 rows to 4in (10cm) over garter stitch using US 5 (3.75mm) needles.

Abbreviations
See page 17.

Knitting notes The body of the cardigan is made in one piece and is knitted sideways—from the right front edge to the left front edge. The fluffy yarn knits up very quickly and also helps to disguise less-than-neat seams if you are a beginner knitter.

Pattern

Back and Fronts (made in one piece)

With US 5 (3.75mm) needles, cast on 42(45:48) sts.

Work in garter stitch (knit every row) until work measures 2(2:2¼)in (5(5:6)cm) from cast-on edge, ending with RS facing.

Shape right front neck

Next row (RS): Cast on 3 sts, k to end. *45(48:51) sts*

Next row: Knit.

Next row: Cast on 4 sts, k to end. *49(52:55) sts*

Cont in garter stitch without further increases until work measures 5½(6:6¼)in (14(15:16)cm) from cast-on edge, ending with RS facing.

Make first armhole

Next row: Bind (cast) off 24(26:28) sts, k to end. *25(26:27) sts*

Next row: K to end, turn and cast on 24(26:28) sts. *49(52:55) sts*

Cont in garter stitch with no further shaping until work measures 2¾(3½:4)in (7(9:10)cm) from armhole, ending with RS facing.

Shape back neck

Next row: Bind (cast) off 3 sts, k to end. *46(49:52) sts*

Cont in garter stitch until work measures 8(8:8¼)in (20(20:21)cm) from armhole, ending with RS facing.

Next row: Cast on 3 sts, k to end. *49(52:55) sts*

Cont in garter stitch until work measures 10¾(11½:12¼)in (27(29:31)cm) from armhole, ending with RS facing.

Make second armhole

Next row: Bind (cast) off 24(26:28) sts, k to end. *25(26:27) sts*

Next row: K to end, turn and cast on 24(26:28) sts. *49(52:55) sts*

Cont in garter stitch with no further shaping until work measures 3½(4:4)in (9(10:10)cm) from armhole, ending with RS facing.

Shape left front neck

Next row: Bind (cast) off 4 sts, k to end. *45(48:51) sts*

Next row: Knit.

Next row: Bind (cast) off 3 sts, k to end. *42(45:48) sts*

Cont in garter stitch with no further shaping until Left Front matches Right Front.

Bind (cast) off.

Sleeves (make two)

Cast on 35(36:39) sts and, working in garter stitch, inc 1 at each end of 5th(3rd:5th) and every foll 7th row until there are 49(52:55) sts.

Cont without further shaping until work measures 5(5½:6)in (13(14:15)cm) from cast-on edge.

Bind (cast) off.

Cord tie (make two)
With US 3 (3.25mm) double-pointed needles, cast on 3 sts
Row 1: K3, do not turn but slide sts to other end of needle.
Rep row 1, pulling yarn tightly across back of work, until work measures
11³/₄in (30cm).
Bind (cast) off.

Collar
Join shoulder seams.
With RS facing and beg at top of right front edge, pick up and k 11(11:12) sts
across lower edge of neckline, 9 sts up right front neck to shoulder seam, 3 sts
down right back neck, 22(22:24) sts across back, 3 sts up left back neck to
shoulder seam, 9 sts down left front neck, and 11(11:12) sts across.
68(68:72) sts
Work in garter stitch for 11(12:13) rows.
Bind (cast) off.

To finish
Weave in any loose ends neatly.
Matching shoulder seam to center of bound-off (cast-off) row, stitch sleeves
in place. Stitch sleeve seams. Sew one cord to each neck edge below collar on
RS. Make 2 pom-poms 1¹/₄in (3cm) and attach 1 to end of each cord.

cardigan with frill

Made from soft, silky bamboo yarn, this loose-fitting cardigan is a great spring and summer cover-up for when the sun disappears behind a cloud. The cute frilled hem makes it pretty enough for a party.

Yarn

6 x 1³⁄₄oz (50g) balls—approx 624yds (570m)—of Sirdar Snuggly Baby Bamboo DK in shade 151 Pom Pom

Needles

Pair each of US 3 (3.25mm) and US 2 (2.75mm) knitting needles

Extras

Tapestry needle
6 x ½in (13mm) buttons
Sewing needle
Sewing thread to match yarn

Sizes

2–3 years

Actual size

Around chest: 26³⁄₄in (68cm)
Shoulder to hem: 14¹⁄₄in (36cm)
Sleeve seam: 9³⁄₄in (25cm)

Gauge (tension)

21 sts and 25 rows to 4in (10cm) over stockinette (stocking) stitch using US 3 (3.25mm) needles.

Abbreviations

See page 17.

Pattern

Back

With US 3 (3.25mm) needles, cast on 261 sts.
Row 1: K1, [bind (cast) off 4, then k10 (11 sts on needle after bind (cast) off)] to last 5 sts, bind (cast) off 5. *188 sts*
Row 2: [K9, k2tog] to last st, k1. *171 sts*
Row 3: K1, [p1, k1] to end.
Row 4: K1, p1, *[k1, p1] 3 times, k1, sk2po, rep from * to last 9 sts, [k1, p1] 4 times, k1. *139 sts*

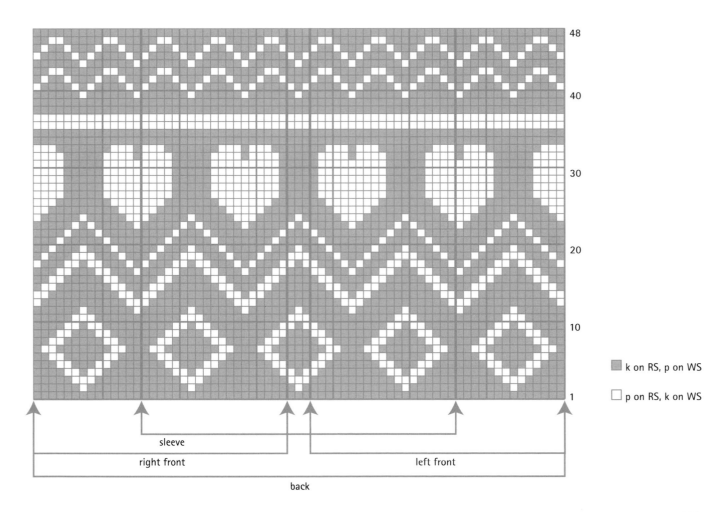

k on RS, p on WS
p on RS, k on WS

sleeve

right front

left front

back

Row 5: K1, [p1, k1] to end
Rep row 5, 5 times more.
Row 11: K1, [k2tog] to last 2 sts, k2. *71 sts*
Row 12: Dec 1, k to last 2 sts, dec 1. *69 sts*
Row 13: Knit.
Row 14: Knit
Row 15: Purl. Work rows 1 to 48 of chart, then rep rows 1 to 34.
Bind (cast) off.

Left front
With US 3 (3.25mm) needles, cast on 126 sts.
Row 1: K1, [bind (cast) off 4, then k10 (11 sts on needle after bind (cast) off)]
to last 5 sts, bind (cast) off 5 sts. *89 sts*
Row 2: [K9, k2tog] to last st, k1. *81 sts*
Row 3: K1, [p1, k1] to end
Row 4: K1, p1, *[k1, p1] 3 times, k1, sk2po, rep from * to last 9 sts, [k1, p1]
4 times, k1. *67 sts*
Row 5: K1, [p1, k1] to end.
Rep row 5, 5 times more.
Row 11: K1, [k2tog] to end. *34 sts*
Row 12: Dec 1, k to end. *33 sts*
Place marker at end of row.
Row 13: Knit.
Row 14: Knit.
Row 15: Purl.
Work rows 1 to 48 of chart, then rep rows 1 to 17, ending with a RS row.
Shape neck
Still continuing to work patt from chart, bind (cast) off 5 sts at beg of next
row, then work to end. *28 sts*
Dec 1 st at neck edge on next row and foll 4 alt rows. *23 sts*
Cont working from chart, without further shaping, until Front measures the
same as Back.
Bind (cast) off.

Right front
Work as for Left Front, but reversing shaping.

Sleeves (make two)
With US 2 (2.75mm) needles, cast on 35 sts.
Row 1: K1, [p1, k1] to end.
Row 2: P1, [k1, p1] to end.
Rep these 2 rows once more, then rep row 1 once.

Row 6: Rib 5, [M1, rib 5] to end. *41 sts*
Change to US 3 (3.25mm) needles.
Row 7: Knit.
Row 8: Purl.
Work rows 1 to 34 of chart, at the same time inc 1 at each end of rows 10, 17, 24, and 31.
Beg with a knit row, cont in stockinette (stocking) stitch, inc 1 at each end of next and every foll 4th row until there are 59 sts.
Cont without further shaping until sleeve measures 9¾in (25cm) from cast-on edge.
Bind (cast) off.

Buttonhole band
With RS of work facing, using US 2 (2.75mm) needles, and starting at marker, pick up and knit 60 sts up right front edge.
Row 1: [K1, p1] to end.
Row 2: (buttonhole): K1, [yo, k2tog, rib 8] 5 times, yo, k2tog, rib 7.
Rep row 1, 3 times more.
Bind (cast) off in rib.

Button band
With RS of work facing, using US 2 (2.75mm) needles, and ending at marker, pick up and knit 60 sts down left front edge.
Row 1: [P1, k1] to end.
Rep row 1, 4 times more.
Bind (cast) off in rib.

Collar
Join shoulder seams.
With RS of work facing, using US 2 (2.75mm) needles, and beg at center of buttonhole band, pick up and knit 24 sts up right front neck, 23 sts across back neck, and 24 sts down left front to center of button band. *71 sts*
Row 1: P1, [k1, p1] to end.
Row 2: K1, [p1, k1] to end.
Rep rows 1–2, 4 times more.
Bind (cast) off in rib.

To finish
Weave in any loose ends neatly.
Matching center of bound-off (cast-off) edge of sleeve to shoulder seam, stitch sleeves in place, then stitch underarm and side seams.
Sew on buttons to correspond with buttonholes.

• bloomers • dungarees • short-sleeved smock
• little leggings • daisy skirt

chapter three

skirts, dresses, and pants

bloomers

For a baby boy or girl, these cute shorts are simple to knit. They are made in two pieces—front and back, both the same—and will easily accommodate a bulky nappy.

Yarn

3(3:4) x 1¾oz (50g) balls—approx 312(312:416)yds (285(285:380)m)—of Sirdar Snuggly Baby Bamboo DK in shade 071 shell pink

Needles

Pair each of US 3 (3.25mm) and US 6 (4.00mm) knitting needles

Extras

Stitch holder

Tapestry needle

59in (1.5m) cord elastic

Sizes

6(9:12) months

Actual size

Width: 11½(12½:13)in (29(32:33)cm) (measured flat between straight side seams)

Length to waistband: 10½(11½:12¼)in (26.5(29:31)cm)

Gauge (tension)

22 sts and 31 rows to 4in (10cm) over stockinette (stocking) stitch using US 6 (4.00mm) needles.

Abbreviations

See page 17.

Knitting notes To make the waistband fit snugly, insert cord elastic under one or two rows of the ribbing on the inside.

Pattern

Front and back (both alike)

**With US 6 (4.00mm) needles, cast on 36(38:40) sts.

Beg with a k row, work in stockinette (stocking) stitch (1 row knit, 1 row purl) until work measures 1¾(2:2¼)in (4.5(5:5.5)cm) from cast-on edge, ending with a purl row.**

Do not bind (cast) off but cut yarn and leave sts on a stitch holder.

Rep from ** to **.

Next row: K to end, then knit stitches from stitch holder. *72(76:80) sts*

Next row: Purl.

Next row: K32(34:36), k3tog, k2, sk2po, k32(34:36). *68(72:76) sts*

Next row: Purl.

Next row: K31(33:35), k2tog, k2, skpo, k31(33:35). *66(70:74) sts*

Next row: Purl.

Next row: K30(32:34), k2tog, k2, skpo, k30(32:34). *64(68:72) sts*

Cont in stockinette (stocking) stitch until work measures 9¾(10¾:11½)in (25(27:29)cm) from cast-on edge, ending with a knit row.

Next row (WS): P3(1:3), *p2tog, p2, rep from * to last 5(3:5) sts, p2tog, p3(1:3). *49(51:55) sts*

Waistband

Change to US 3 (3.25mm) needles.

Row 1: K1, [p1, k1] to end.

Row 2: P1, [k1, p1] to end.

Rep rows 1–2 twice more.

Bind (cast) off in rib.

Leg borders

Join side seams.

With right side of work facing and using US 3 (3.25mm) needles, pick up and knit 49(53:57) sts around the bottom of one leg (cast-on edges) and work in rib as folls:

Row 1: K1, [p1, k1] to end.

Row 2: P1, [k1, p1] to end.

Rep rows 1–2 twice more.

Bind (cast) off in rib.

Work border on other leg to match.

To finish

Weave in any loose ends neatly.

Stitch inner leg seam.

dungarees

A classic choice for little boys, these bib-and-brace trousers are cute, warm, and practical. Little girls will love them, too, so be prepared to knit them in pretty colors.

Yarn
4(5:6) x 1¾oz (50g) balls—approx 508(635:762)yds (464(580:696)m)—of Sublime Baby Cashmere Merino Silk DK in shade 0161 Lulu

Needles
Pair each of US 3 (3.25mm) and US 6 (4.00mm) knitting needles

Extras
Stitch holder
Tapestry needle
2 x ⅝in (15mm) buttons
Sewing needle
Sewing thread to match yarn

Size
6(9:12) months

Actual size
Waist: 20½(22:23½)in (52(56:59.5)cm)
Waist to ankle, with ankle rib folded: 14¾(16½:18)in (37.5(42:46)cm)

Gauge (tension)
22 sts and 31 rows to 4in (10cm) over stockinette (stocking) stitch using US 6 (4.00mm) needles.

Abbreviations
See page 17.

Pattern

Right leg

**With US 3 (3.25mm) needles, cast on 59(63:67) sts.
Row 1(RS): K1, [p1, k1] to end.
Row 2: P1, [k1, p1] to end.
Rep rows 1–2 until work measures 2½in (6cm) from cast-on edge.
Change to US 6 (4.00mm) needles.
Next row (RS): K3(4:5), * inc 1 in each of next 2 sts, k 1, rep from * to last to last 5 sts, inc 1, k4. *94(100:106) sts*
Next row: Purl.
Beg with a k row, work in stockinette (stocking) stitch (1 row knit, 1 row purl) with no further shaping for 46(52:58) rows.
Next row: Bind (cast) off 2 sts at beg of next 2 rows and 1 st at beg of next 6 rows.**
Do not bind (cast) off but cut yarn and leave sts on a stitch holder.

Left leg

Work as for Right Leg from ** to **.

Next row: K to end, then pick up and k stitches of Right Leg from stitch holder. *168(180:192) sts*

Cont in stockinette (stocking) stitch for a further 48(54:60) rows.

Next row (WS): P2, *p2tog, p1, rep from * to last st, p1. *113(121:129) sts*

Waistband

Change to US 3 (3.25mm) needles.

Next row (RS): K1, [p1, k1] to end.

Next row: P1, [k1, p1] to end.

Rep these 2 rows twice more.

Next row: [K1, p1] 18(19:21) times, turn and bind (cast) off these 36(38:42) sts in rib.

Cut yarn and rejoin to rem sts, k1, [p1, k1] 3 times and transfer these 7 sts to a stitch holder (for Left Strap), then p1, [k1, p1] 16(18:18) times, k1 and transfer the last 7 sts worked on to a stitch holder (for Right Strap), [p1, k1] to end, turn and bind (cast) off 36(38:42) sts.

Cut yarn.

Bib

With wrong side facing, rejoin yarn to 27(31:31) sts at center front and, with US 6 (4.00mm) needles and beg with a purl row, work 23(29:31) rows in stockinette (stocking) stitch.

Change to US 3 (3.25mm) needles.

Next row (RS): K1, [p1, k1] to end.

Next row: P1, [k1, p1] to end.

Rep last 2 rows once more then bind (cast) off in rib.

Straps

With wrong side facing and using US 3 (3.25mm) needles, rejoin yarn to stitches on stitch holder for Left Strap.

Left strap

Row 1 (WS): P1, [k1, p1] 3 times.

Row 2: K1, [p1, k1] 3 times.

Rep rows 1–2 until strap measures 11¾(13:14¼)in (30(33:36)cm) from cast-on edge, ending with a WS row.

Next row (buttonhole): K1, p1, yo twice, sl1 knitwise, k2tog, psso, p1, k1.

Next row: As row 1.

Bind (cast) off.

Right strap

With wrong side facing and using US 3 (3.25mm) needles, rejoin yarn to stitches on stitch holder for Right Strap.

Work as for Left Strap.

To finish

Weave in any loose ends neatly.

Stitch center seam between legs. Join inner leg seams, reversing seam on ribbing. Turn up ribbing at ankles to form a cuff.

Stitch inner edge of each strap to sides of bib. Stitch buttons to back waistband.

Knitting notes If you wish, you can omit the bib and braces and simply work 6 rows of ribbing at the waistband, to make knitted trousers. To make the waistband fit snugly, insert cord elastic under one or two rows of the ribbing on the inside.

short-sleeved smock

Bright pink is a favorite with little girls so this smock, with a zingy zigzag stripe across the yoke, is sure to please.

Yarn

4(5) x 1³⁄₄oz (50g) balls—approx 508(635)yds (464(580)m)—of Sublime Baby Cashmere Merino Silk DK in shade 162 Pinkaboo (A) and 1 ball—approx 127yds (116m)—in each of shade 158 Ladybug (B) and shade 48 Cheeky (C)

Needles

Pair each of US 6 (4.00mm) and US 3 (3.25mm) knitting needles
US 6 (4.00mm) circular knitting needle, 24in (60cm) long

Extras

4 stitch holders (one large, three small)
Tapestry needle
3 x ¹⁄₂in (12mm) buttons
Sewing needle
Sewing thread to match yarn

Sizes

1(2) years

Actual size

Shoulder to hem: 12¹⁄₄(13¹⁄₂)in (31(34)cm)
Width across back: 10¹⁄₄(10¹⁄₂)in (26(26.5)cm)
Sleeve seam: 2¹⁄₄(2¹⁄₄)in (5.5(5.5)cm)

Gauge (tension)

22 sts and 29 rows to 4in (10cm) over stockinette (stocking) stitch using US 6 (4.00mm) needles.

Abbreviations

See page 17.

See page 17.

Knitting notes When you have cast on to make the main part of the dress, you will have a lot of stitches on your needle. Though the skirt is knitted in the round, it is advisable to work the first few rows back and forth, as you would on a pair of knitting needles, to avoid the work becoming twisted. You can then carry on knitting in the round to produce a seamless tube of fabric. Sew up the tiny bit of open seam at the bottom of the skirt when you have completed the knitting.

When you divide the work for the front and back yoke, you can continue to use the circular needle, working back and forth, or change to a pair of straight needles if you prefer.

If the idea of knitting the zigzag motif on the front yoke is too daunting, for a simpler version you could work three stripes of two rows each in contrasting colors. Or, of course, you can omit pattern altogether and knit six rows in the main color instead.

Pattern

Dress

With US 6 (4.00mm) circular needle and yarn A, cast on 168(172) sts.
Rounds 1–6: Knit.
Round 7 (picot hem): [Yo, k2tog] to end of round.
Cont in stockinette (stocking) stitch (knit every round) until work measures 8¹⁄₄(9)in (21(23)cm) from cast-on edge.
Next round: [K1, k2tog] to last 0(1) st, k0(1). *112(115) sts*
Work 4 rounds in stockinette (stocking) stitch with no further decreases.

Shape armholes

Next row: Bind (cast) off 3 sts, k until there are 53(54) sts on RH needle and turn, leaving rem sts on a holder.
Next row: Bind (cast) off 3 sts, p to end. *50(51) sts*
Dec 1 st at each end of the next and every alt row until 44(45) sts rem.
Work 3(5) rows in stockinette (stocking) stitch (1 row knit, 1 row purl), ending with RS facing.

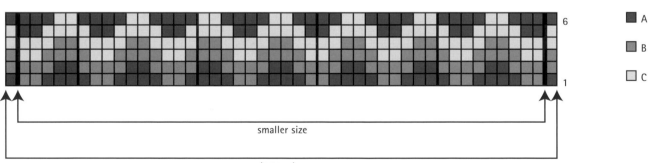

6

1

■ A

■ B

□ C

smaller size

larger size

Back opening

Next row: K24(25) and turn, leaving rem sts on a holder for Left Back.

Next row: K5, p to end.

Next row: Knit.

Next row: K5, p to end.

Next row (buttonhole): K to last 3 sts, yo, k2tog, k1.

Next row: K5, p to end.

Next row: Knit.

Next row: K5, p to end.

Rep last 2 rows 3 times more.

Next row (buttonhole): K to last 3 sts, yo, k2tog, k1.

Next row: K5, p to end.

Next row: Knit.

Next row: K5, p to end.

Rep last 2 rows once more.

Shape shoulder

Next row: Bind (cast) off 3 sts, k to end.

Next row: K5, p to end.

Rep last 2 rows once more.

Next row (buttonhole): Bind (cast) off 4 sts, k to last 3 sts, yo, k2tog, k1.

Next row: K5, p to end.

Leave the rem 14(15) sts on a holder.

With RS facing, join yarn to 20 sts on holder for left back and cast on 4(5) sts, k these sts then k to end. *24(25) sts*

Next row: P to last 5 sts, k5.

Next row: Knit.

Rep last 2 rows 9 times more.

Shape shoulder

Next row: Bind (cast) off 3 sts, p to last 5 sts, k5.

Next row: Knit.

Rep last 2 rows once more.

Next row: Bind (cast) off 4 sts, p to last 5 sts, k5.

Next row: Knit.

Leave the rem 14(15) sts on a holder.

Front

With RS facing, join yarn to 56 (58) sts on holder for front.

Next row: Bind (cast) off 3 sts, k to end. *53(55) sts*

Next row: Bind (cast) off 3 sts, p to end. *50(52) sts*

Dec 1 st at each end of next and foll 2 alt rows. *44(46) sts*

Next row: Work 3(5) rows with no further shaping.

Work next 6 rows from chart, joining in yarns B and C as indicated, then work 4 rows in yarn A.

Shape neck

Next row: K15 and turn, leaving rem 29(31) sts on a holder.

Next row: P1, p2tog, p to end.

Next row: K to last 3 sts, k2tog, k1.

Rep last 2 rows once more. 11 sts

Next row: P1, p2tog, p to end.

Work 4 rows with no further decreases, ending at armhole edge.

Shape shoulder

Bind (cast) off 3 sts, k to end.

Next row: Purl.

Rep last 2 rows once more.

Bind (cast) off rem 4 sts.

Keeping the center 14(16) sts on the stitch holder, join yarn to rem 15 sts for Right Front Neck and k to end.

Complete to match Left Front Neck, but reversing shaping.

Sleeves (make two)

Using US 3 (3.25mm) needles and yarn A, cast on 40(42) sts.

Beg with a knit row, work 4 rows in stockinette (stocking) stitch.

Next row (picot hem): K1, [yo, k2tog] to last st, k1.

Work a further 3 rows in stockinette (stocking) stitch.

Change to US 6 (4.00mm) needles.

Cont in stockinette (stocking) stitch, inc 1 at each end of 5th and foll 6th row. *44(46) sts*

Next row: Purl.

Next row: Bind (cast) off 4 sts, k to end.

Next row: Bind (cast) off 4 sts, p to end.

Dec 1 st at each end of next row and then on every foll 4th row until 30(32) sts rem.

Dec 1st at each end of every row until 12(14) sts rem.

Bind (cast) off.

Neckband

Stitch shoulder seams.

With RS facing, using US 3 (3.25mm) needles and yarn A, k 14(15) sts from holder for left back neck, then pick up and knit 13 sts down left side of neck, k 14(16) sts from holder at center front neck, pick up and knit 13 sts up right side of neck, and k 14(15) sts from holder at right back neck. *68(72) sts*

Starting with a purl row, work 3 rows in stockinette (stocking) stitch.

Next row (picot hem): K1, [yo, k2tog] to last st, k1.

Beg with a purl row, work a further 3 rows in stockinette (stocking) stitch.

Bind (cast) off.

To finish

Weave in any loose ends neatly.

Stitch sleeve seams and stitch sleeves to armhole edges, matching end of shoulder seam to center of cast-off edge on sleeve.

Fold picot hems to inside on lower edge of skirt, sleeves, and neck and slip stitch in place.

At back, with buttonhole edge uppermost, stitch lower edges together, then sew on buttons to correspond with buttonholes.

little leggings

Leggings with feet are great for a ride in the pram or pushchair, while the
footless version is ideal for older babies starting to crawl or walk.

Yarn

3 x 1¾oz (50g) balls—approx 369yds (339m)—of Rowan Wool Cotton DK in shade 968 Cypress or 941 Clear

Needles

Pair each of US 2 (3.00mm) and US 5 (3.75mm) knitting needles

2 US 3 (3.25mm) double-pointed knitting needles

Extras

2 stitch holders (small)

Tapestry needle

Sizes

3-6(9-12) months

Actual size

Back waist to ankle: 16¾(17¾)in (42.5(45)cm)

Around waist: 21¾(23¼)in (55(59)cm)

Gauge (tension)

21 sts and 27 rows to 4in (10cm) over stockinette (stocking) stitch using US 5 (3.75mm) needles.

Abbreviations

See page 17.

Pattern

Right leg

**With US 2 (3.00mm) needles, cast on 57(61) sts.

Row 1: K1, [p1, k1] to end.

Row 2: P1, [k1, p1 to end.

Rep rows 1–2 twice more.

Row 7: K1, * yo, k2tog, p1, k1, rep from * to end.

Row 8: P1, [k1, p1] to end.

Row 9: K1, [p1, k1] to end.

Rep rows 8–9 once more, then row 8 once more.

Change to US 5 (3.75mm) needles.

Row 13: Knit.

Row 14: Purl.**

Shape back

Row 15 (RS): K11(12), turn.

Row 16 and 3 foll WS rows: P to end.

Row 17: K17(18), turn.

Row 19: K23(24), turn.

Row 21: K29(30), turn.

Row 23: K35(36), turn.

Row 24: P to end.

Beg with a k row, work in stockinette (stocking) stitch (1 row knit, 1 row purl), inc 1 at beg of 5th and every foll 8th row until there are 61(65) sts.

Cont without further shaping until front (unshaped) side measures 7(7½)in (18(19)cm) from cast-on edge, ending with a purl row.

Shape leg

***Cont in stockinette (stocking) stitch, dec 1 st at each end of next and every alt row 5(6) times, until 49(51) sts rem, then at each end of every foll 4th row 7(8) times. *35 sts*

Cont in stockinette (stocking) stitch without further shaping until front side of work measures 14½(15½)in (36.5(39.5)cm) from cast-on edge, ending with a purl row.

Change to US 2 (3.00mm) needles.

Next row: K1, [p1, k1] to end.

Next row: P1, [k1, p1] to end.

Rep last 2 rows twice more.

For footless leggings

Work a further 4 rows in rib.

Bind (cast) off in rib.

For leggings with feet

Change to US 5 (3.75mm) needles and proceed as folls:

Next row: Knit.

Next row: Purl.***

Next row: K28, turn and leave rem 7 sts on a holder.

Next row: P11, turn and leave rem 17 sts on holder.

Beg with a knit row, work 16(18) rows in stockinette (stocking) stitch on these 11 sts. Cut yarn.

With right side facing, rejoin yarn and knit 17 sts on holder, then pick up and knit 10(11) sts along right side of work, k11 sts on needle, pick up and knit 10(11) sts down opposite side, and then knit 7 sts from holder. *55(57) sts*

Beg with a purl row, work 9 rows in stockinette (stocking) stitch.

Shape sole

Row 1: K3, k2tog, skpo, k19(20), skpo, k9, k2tog, k16(17).

Row 2: Knit.

Row 3: K2, k2tog, skpo, k19(20), skpo, k7, k2tog, k15(16).

Row 4: Knit.

Row 5: K1, k2tog, skpo, k19(20), skpo, k5, k2tog, k14(15). *43(45) sts*

Bind (cast) off.

Left leg

Work as for Right Leg from ** to **.

Shape back

Row 15 and 4 foll RS rows: K to end.

Row 16: P11(12), turn.

Row 18: P17(18), turn.

Row 20: P23(24), turn.

Row 22: P29(30), turn.

Row 24: P35(36), turn.

Cont in stockinette (stocking) stitch, inc 1 at beg of 5th and every foll 8th row until there are 61(65) sts.

Cont without further shaping until front (unshaped) side measures 7(7½)in (18(19)cm) from cast-on edge, ending with a purl row.

Shape leg

Work as for Left Leg from *** to ***.

Next row: K18, turn and leave rem 17 sts on a holder.

Next row: P11, turn and leave rem 7 sts on holder.

Beg with a knit row, work 16(18) rows in stockinette (stocking) stitch on these 11 sts. Cut yarn.

With right side facing, rejoin yarn and knit 7 sts on holder, then pick up and knit 10(11) sts up right side of work, k11 sts on needle, pick up and knit 10(11) sts down opposite side, and then knit 17 sts from holder. *55(57) sts*

Beg with a purl row, work 9 rows in stockinette (stocking) stitch.

Shape sole

Row 1: K16(17), skpo, k9, k2tog, k19(20), k2tog, skpo, k3.

Row 2: Knit.

Row 3: K15(16), skpo, k7, k2tog, k19(20), k2tog, skpo, k2.

Row 4: Knit.

Row 5: K14(15), skpo, k5, k2tog, k19(20), k2tog, skpo, k1.

Bind (cast) off.

Cord tie

With US 3 (3.25mm) double-pointed needles, cast on 2 sts.

Row 1: K2, do not turn but slide sts to other end of needle.

Rep row 1, pulling yarn tightly across back of work, until work measures 37½(41½)in (95(105)cm).

Bind (cast) off.

To finish

Weave in any loose ends neatly.

Stitch front, back, and inside leg seams then stitch foot seams.

Thread cord through eyelets at waist and knot ends.

Knitting notes For leggings with or without feet, the basic pattern is the same: just bind (cast) off after the rib when making the footless version. A great garment for boys and girls, you'll knit lots of these in different colors.

daisy skirt

This soft skirt features a border of daisies to add a bright touch to any day. The deep picot hem covers up the strands of thread on the inside, while the soft ribbed waistband is elasticated for a snug fit. The fullness of the skirt, which is knitted in one seamless piece, means it's perfect for twirling.

Yarn
4(4:5) x 1¾oz (50g) balls—approx 436(436:545)yds (400(400:500)m)—of Rowan Baby Alpaca DK in shade 219 Cute (A)
1(1:1) x 1¾oz (50g) ball—approx 123yds (113m)—of Rowan Wool Cotton in shade 946 Elf (B)
1(1:1) x 1¾oz (50g) ball—approx 109yds (100m)—of Rowan Silk Wool DK in each of shade 300 Milk (C), and shade 316 Citronelle (D)

Needles
US 3 (3.25mm) circular knitting needle, 24in (60cm) or 32in (80cm) long
US 2 (2.75mm) circular knitting needle, 16in (40cm) long

Extras
Tapestry needle
20½in (52cm) elastic, ½in (12mm) wide

Sizes
1(2:3) years

Actual size
Waist: 19½(20¼:21)in (49.5(51.5:53)cm)
Length to waistband: 7½(9¼:11½)in (19(23.5:29)cm)

Gauge (tension)
22 sts and 29 rows to 4in (10cm) over stockinette (stocking) stitch using US 3 (3.25mm) needles.

Abbreviations
See page 17.

Knitting notes If knitting the flower border seems too time-consuming or beyond your skill level, you could omit it and knit 12 plain rows instead. When working in the round on a circular needle, work the first few rows after the cast-on row back and forth (one row knit, one row purl), as the knitted fabric has a tendency to become twisted. After a few rows, begin working in rounds. When making up, close the small gap at the start of the work with a few neat stitches.

Pattern

Skirt

With US 3 (3.25mm) needle and yarn A, cast on 270(280:290) sts.

Rounds 1–14: Knit.

Round 15 (picot hem): [Yo, k2tog] to end of round.

Rounds 16-17: Knit.

Follow chart for flower border.

Cont in yarn A, knit 2(5:8) rounds.

Next round: [K8, skpo] to end of round. *243(252:261) sts*

Knit 10(14:18) rounds.

Next round: [K7, skpo] to end of round. *216(224:232) sts*

Knit 9(10:14) rounds.

Next round: [K6, skpo] to end of round. *189(196:203) sts*

Knit 7(8:10) rounds.

Next round: [K5, skpo] to end of round. *162(168:174) sts*

Knit 4(6:8) rounds.

Next round: [K4, skpo] to end of round. *135(140:145) sts*

Knit 2(4:6) rounds.

Next round: [K3, skpo] to end of round. *108(112:116) sts*

Waistband

Change to US 2 (2.75mm) needles and work in k1, p1 rib for 15 rounds.

Bind (cast) off in rib.

To finish

Weave in any loose ends neatly.

Fold hem to wrong side at picot row and slip stitch in place.

Fold ribbing in half to wrong side and slip stitch bound-off (cast-off) edge to first row of ribbing, leaving a small gap. Cut a length of elastic measuring 19(19³/4:20¹/2)in (48(50:52)cm), or to fit child's waist, insert into waistband, overlap ends by ¹/2in (1cm) and stitch. Slip stitch opening in waistband closed.

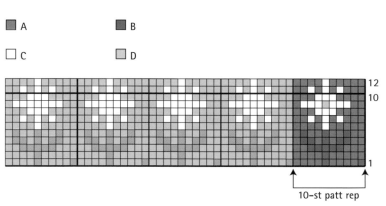

☐ A   ☐ B

☐ C   ☐ D

10-st patt rep

• lacy bootees • lacy mittens • traditional bonnet
• chunky hat • soft shoes • fair isle beanie

chapter four

outdoor warmers

lacy bootees

Pretty bootees are always a welcome gift for a newborn baby. These are designed to completely enclose the feet, keeping them warm and cozy, and the lacy legs will keep ankles cozy, too. Ribbon ties help to keep the bootees from falling off.

Yarn
1 x 1¾oz (50g) ball—approx 230yds (210m)—of Regia Silk 4-ply in shade 01 white

Needles
Pair of US 3 (3.00mm) knitting needles

Extras
2 stitch holders
Tapestry needle
35½in (90cm) of ⅜-in (10-mm) wide silk or satin ribbon

Size
Newborn

Actual size
Foot length: 4⅛in (10.5cm)
Cuff to base of heel: 3¼in (8cm)

Gauge (tension)
30 sts and 50 rows to 4in (10cm) over stockinette (stocking) stitch using US 3 (3.00mm) needles.

Abbreviations
See page 17.

Pattern

Bootee (make two)
With US 3 (3.00mm) needles, cast on 41 sts.
Knit 2 rows.
Row 3 (RS): P1, [k3, p1] to end.
Row 4: K1, [p3, k1] to end.
Row 5: [P1, k1, yo, skpo] to last st, p1.
Row 6: As row 4.
Rep rows 3–6, 3 times more.
Next row: K2, [k2tog, k5] to last 4 sts, k2tog, k2. *35 sts*
Next row: Purl.
Next row (eyelets): K2, [yo, k2tog] to last st, k1.
Next row: Purl.
Shape top of foot
Next row: K23, turn and leave rem 12 sts on a holder.

Next row: P11, turn and leave rem 12 sts on a second holder.
Next row: Starting with a knit row, work in stockinette (stocking) stitch (1 row knit, 1 row purl) on these 11 sts until work measures 2in (5cm), ending with a purl row. Cut yarn
Knit 12 sts from second holder, then pick up and k 16 sts evenly along the side of the top of the foot you have just worked, then k 11 sts on needle, then pick up and k 16 sts down other side of top of foot, then k 12 sts from first holder. *67 sts*
Beg with a purl row, work in stockinette (stocking) stitch for 9 rows.
Shape sole
Next row (RS): K2, skpo, k26, k2tog, k3, skpo, k26, k2tog, k2. *63 sts*
Next and every alt row: Purl.
Next row: K2, skpo, k24, k2tog, k3, skpo, k24, k2tog, k2. *59 sts*
Next row: K2, skpo, k22, k2tog, k3, skpo, k22, k2tog, k2. *55 sts*
Next row: K2, skpo, k20, k2tog, k3, skpo, k20, k2tog, k2. *51 sts*
Bind (cast) off purlwise.

To finish

Join back seam and foot seam.
Weave in any loose ends neatly.
Cut ribbon in half and thread through eyelets.

Knitting notes *One ball of this yarn is more than enough to make these bootees and the mittens on page 64, so why not make a matching set as a gift? If you are feeling particularly generous, the bonnet on page 66 is also made using the same yarn.*

lacy mittens

Designed to match the bootees on page 62, these little mittens not only keep baby's hands warm but help to prevent scratching, too. Add ribbons in your own choice of color.

Knitting notes *The cuffs of these mittens are made in exactly the same way as the lacy legs of the bootees on page 62, so they make a good set. For shorter cuffs, work fewer rows (rep the four patt rows once or twice instead of three times).*

Yarn
1 x 1¾oz (50g) ball—approx 230yds (210m)—of Regia Silk 4-ply in shade 01 white

Needles
Pair of US 3 (3.00mm) knitting needles

Extras
Tapestry needle
31½in (80cm) of ⅜-in (10-mm) wide silk or satin ribbon

Size
Newborn

Actual size
Overall length: 4½in (11.5cm)
Width: 2¼in (5.5cm)

Gauge (tension)
30 sts and 50 rows to to 4in (10cm) over stockinette (stocking) stitch using US 3 (3.00mm) needles.

Abbreviations
See page 17.

Pattern

Mitten (make two)
With US 3 (3.00mm) needles, cast on 41 sts.
Knit 2 rows.
Row 3 (RS): P1, [k3, p1] to end.
Row 4: K1, [p3, k1] to end.
Row 5: [P1, k1, yo, skpo] to last st, p1.
Row 6: As row 4.
Rep rows 3-6, 3 times morc.
Next row: K2, [k2tog, k5] to last 4 sts, k2tog, k2. *35 sts*
Next row: Purl.
Next row (make eyelets): K2, [yo, k2tog] to last st, k1. Starting with a purl row, work in stockinette (stocking) stitch (1 row knit, 1 row purl) until work measures 4¼in (10.5cm) from cast-on edge, ending with a purl row.
Next row: K2, *sk2po, k1, rep from * to last 5 sts, sk2po, k2. *19 sts*
Next row: Purl.
Next row: K1, [k2tog] to end. Cut yarn and thread through rem sts.

To finish

Pull end of yarn to draw up stitches, then stitch side seam.
Weave in any loose ends neatly.
Cut ribbon in half and thread through eyelets.

traditional bonnet

This cute bonnet fits comfortably, ties under the chin or to one side of the head, and keeps baby's ears nice and warm. Knit the bootees on page 62 and mittens on page 64 to make a set.

Yarn
1 x 1¾oz (50g) ball—approx 230yds (210m)—of Regia Silk 4-ply in shade 01 white

Needles
Pair each of US 2 (2.75mm) and US 3 (3.00mm) knitting needles

Extras
Tapestry needle
39in (1m) of ¾-in (19-mm) wide silk or satin ribbon
Sewing needle
Sewing thread to match yarn

Size
Newborn

Actual size
Around neck edge: 13½in (34cm)
Center back to front edge: 6¾in (17cm).

Gauge (tension)
30 sts and 50 rows to 4in (10cm) over stockinette (stocking) stitch using US 3 (3.00mm) needles.

Abbreviations
See page 17.

Pattern

Bonnet (made in one piece)
With US 2 (2.75mm) needles, cast on 87 sts.
Row 1: K1, [p1, k1] to end.
Row 2: P1, [k1, p1] to end.
Rep rows 1–2 until ribbing measures 1in (2.5cm) from cast-on edge.
Change to US 3 (3.00mm) needles.
Beg with a knit row, work in stockinette (stocking) stitch (1 row knit, 1 row purl) until work measures 5in (13cm) from cast-on edge, ending with a p row.
Shape back
Next row: Bind (cast) off 30 sts, k to end. *57 sts*
Next row: Bind (cast) off 30 sts, p to end. *27 sts*
Cont in stockinette (stocking) stitch without further shaping until work measures 9in (23cm) from cast-on edge.
Bind (cast) off.

Neck border
Stitch two back seams.
With right sides facing, starting at front left-hand corner, and using US 2 (2.75mm) needles, pick up and k 32 sts along lower edge of left side, 21 sts along edge of back section, and 32 sts along lower edge of right side. *85 sts*
Row 1: K1, [p1, k1] to end.
Row 2: P1, [k1, p1] to end.
Rep rows 1–2, 7 times more.
Bind (cast) off.

To finish
Weave in any loose ends neatly.
Cut ribbon in half and, using sewing needle and sewing thread, sew one piece to each side, on wrong side of neck ribbing, close to where ribbing joins main part of bonnet. Fold ribbing in half to wrong side, enclosing ribbon ends, and using spare yarn stitch bound-off (cast-off) edge to edge of main part of bonnet.

Knitting notes Easy enough for a novice knitter, the bonnet is made in one T-shaped piece, then the neckband is added. The neckband is folded in half to give a soft edge, which is designed to be gentle against a baby's skin. To complement the soft yarn, choose a silky ribbon, such as the antique silk ribbon used here. Blue ribbon is, of course, traditional for a boy, and pink for a girl—but choose any color you like.

chunky hat

Great for keeping out the cold, this chunky hat is quick to knit with no shaping involved. The perky tassels add a touch of fun.

Yarn
2 x 1³/₄oz (50g) balls—approx 110yds (100m)—of Rowan Felted Tweed Chunky in shade 283 Grey Pebble

Needles
Pair each of US 9 (5.50mm) and US 10½ (7.00mm) knitting needles

Extras
Tapestry needle

Sizes
12 months (18 months:2 years:3 years)

Actual size
17¼(18½:19½:21)in (44(47:49.5:53)cm)

Gauge (tension)
13 sts and 17 rows to 4in (10cm) over stockinette (stocking) stitch using US 10 (7.00mm) needles.

Abbreviations
See page 17.

See page 17.

Knitting notes This is the simplest possible way to make a hat: you do little more than knit a rectangle and fold it in half, so you will find it a good way of using up leftover yarn. Instead of using chunky yarn, you could try combining thinner yarns to create a chunky effect.

Pattern

Hat

With US 9 (5.50mm) needles, cast on 56(60:64:68) sts
Row 1: [K1, p1] to end.
Rep this 2 row 7(7:9:9) times more.
Change to US 10½ (7.00mm) needles and, beg with a knit row, work in stockinette (stocking) stitch (1 row knit, 1 row purl) for 22(24:25:26) rows.
Bind (cast) off.
Cut yarn.

To finish

With right sides together, stitch edges together to form a tube. Flatten the tube with the seam at center back. Oversew top bound-off (cast-off) edges together. Weave in any loose ends neatly. Fold ribbing in half to wrong side and slip stitch cast-on edge to last row of ribbing. Weave in any loose ends neatly. To make tassels, hold hand flat, fingers together, and wind yarn around four fingers about 30 times. Wrap a short length of yarn around the center of the bundle, tie tightly, then snip loops. Make two tassels and stitch firmly to the top corners of the hat.

soft shoes

Easy to make even for a novice knitter, these shoes are practical as well as pretty, and will always keep baby's toes toasty.

Yarn
1 x 1³/₄oz (50g) ball—approx 127yds (116m)—of Sublime Baby Cashmere Merino Silk DK in shade 03 Vanilla (or shade 124 Splash, or shade 48 Cheeky)

Needles
Pair of US 3 (3.25mm) knitting needles

Extras
Stitch holder
Tapestry needle
2 x ½in (12mm) buttons
Sewing needle
Sewing thread to match yarn

Sizes
3(6:9) months

Actual size
Length: 4(4¼:4½)in (10(10.5:11.5)cm)

Gauge (tension)
22 sts and 40 rows to 4in (10cm) over garter stitch using US 3 (3.25mm) needles.

Abbreviations
See page 17.

Knitting notes *One ball of yarn is enough to make two pairs of shoes. This cashmere and silk blend yarn is the perfect choice as it is so soft next to baby's skin. Make a trio of shoes in an assortment of colors—such as the pink, vanilla, and blue shown here—and buy buttons to match yarn, but switch them around so that the blue shoe has white buttons, the pink shoe has blue buttons, and so on. Pack them with tissue paper in a box for the perfect baby gift.*

Pattern
Shoe (make two)
(made in one piece)
With US 3 (3.25mm) needles, cast on 27(31:35) sts.
Row 1: Knit.
Row 2: K1, inc 1, k10(12:14), inc 1, k1, inc 1, k10(12:14), inc 1, k1. *31(35:39) sts*
Row 3: Knit.
Row 4: K2, inc 1, k10(12:14), inc 1, k3, inc 1, k10(12:14), inc 1, k2. *35(39:43) sts*
Row 5: Knit.
Row 6: K3, inc 1, k10(12:14), inc 1, k5, inc 1, k10(12:14), inc 1, k3. *39(43:47) sts*
Row 7: Knit. Row 8: K4, inc 1, k10(12:14), inc 1, k7, inc 1, k10(12:14), inc 1, k4. *43(47:51) sts*
Knit 7(9:11) rows.
Next row: K13(15:17), [skpo] 4 times, k1 [k2tog] 4 times. k13(15:17). *35(39:43) sts*
Next row: Knit.
Next row: K8(9:10) sts and place on stitch holder, bind (cast) off 19(21:23) sts, then k rem 7(8:9) sts.
Knit 3 rows on these 8(9:10) sts.
Bind (cast) off.

Make strap
Rejoin yarn to end of 8(9:10) sts on holder and cast on 12 sts using cable cast-on. **Next row:** K12, then k8(9:10) sts from holder. *20(21:22) sts*
Next row (buttonhole): K17(18:19), yo, k2tog, k1.
Next row: Knit.
Bind (cast) off.
Make the second shoe with the strap on the other side.

To finish
Weave in any loose ends neatly.
Right sides together, fold shoe in half and stitch back seam. Turn right side out and oversew seam along center of sole.
Using sewing thread, securely stitch button to shoe, on the side opposite the strap.

fair isle beanie

This pull-on beanie hat, featuring a turn-back brim with a traditional Fair Isle pattern, is the perfect winter warmer for little heads.

Yarn
1 x 1³/₄oz (50g) ball—approx 137yds (125m)—of Rowan Pure Wool DK in each of shade 06 Pier (A), shade 12 Snow (B), and shade 08 Marine (C)

Needles
Pair of US 6 (4.00mm) knitting needles

Extras
Tapestry needle

Size
6–12 months

Actual size
Circumference: 20in (51cm)

Gauge (tension)
20 sts and 30 rows to 4in (10cm) over stockinette (stocking) stitch using US 6 (4.00mm) needles.

Abbreviations
See page 17.

Pattern

Hat
With US 6 (4.00mm) needles and yarn A, cast on 100 sts.
Beg with a knit row, work in stockinette (stocking) stitch (1 row knit, 1 row purl) until 13 rows have been worked, ending with a knit row.
Next row (WS): Knit (to create ridge).
Beg with a knit row, work in stockinette (stocking) stitch for 2 rows.
Following chart and joining in yarns B and C as required, work 13 rows of Fair Isle patt, then, starting with a knit row to turn brim, work 8 rows stockinette (stocking) stitch in yarn A, ending with a knit row.
Change to yarn C and, starting with a knit row, work in stockinette (stocking) stitch for 24 rows.
Next row: [K3, k2tog] to end. *80 sts*
Work 3 rows in stockinette (stocking) stitch.
Next row: [K2, k2tog] to end. *60 sts*
Work 3 rows in stockinette (stocking) stitch.
Next row: [K1, k2tog] to end. *40 sts*
Work 1 row in stockinette (stocking) stitch.
Next row: [K2tog] to end. *20 sts*
Next row: [P2tog] to end. *10 sts*
Cut yarn and thread tail of yarn through all sts.

To finish
Stitch edges of work together, ensuring that seam is on wrong side on top section of hat and right side on lower section.
Weave in any loose ends neatly.
Fold plain section of border to wrong side, along garter stitch ridge and slip stitch in place at point where stockinette (stocking) stitch changes to reverse stockinette (stocking) stitch. Fold up brim.

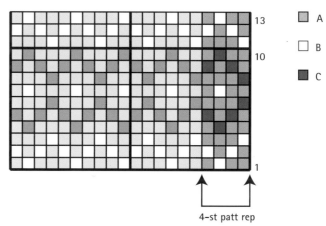

13

10

1

☐ A
☐ B
■ C

4-st patt rep

• square-neck sweater • fisherman's sweater
• jacket with hood • fish sweater • striped jacket

sweaters and jackets

square-neck sweater

Simple yet stylish, this sweater has a square neckline and minimal shaping. For easy dressing and undressing it does up at the back with press fasteners.

Knitting notes Novice knitters are often daunted by instructions for buttonholes and fancy bands. To make things as easy as possible this pattern dispenses with such complications: the back opening features press fasteners. And if picking up stitches around the neckline is a step too far, then leave it unfinished or edge it with blanket stitch using the contrasting color yarn.

Yarn
3(4:4) x 1³/₄oz (50g) balls—approx 381(508:508)yds (348(464:464)m)—of Sublime Baby Cashmere Merino Silk DK in shade 003 Vanilla (A) and 1(1:1) ball—approx 127yds (116m)—in shade 125 Bathtub (B)

Needles
Pair each of US 5 (3.75mm) and US 3 (3.25mm) knitting needles

Extras
1 large and 4 small stitch holders
Tapestry needle
4 press fasteners
Sewing needle
Sewing thread to match yarn

Sizes
3-6(6-9:9-12) months

Actual size
Around chest: 20³/₄(22¹/₂:24)in (52.5(57:61)cm)
Shoulder to hem: 7¹/₄(8¹/₂:9³/₄)in (18.5(21.5:25)cm)
Sleeve seam: 4¹/₂(4³/₄:5¹/₄)in (11.5(12:13.5)cm)

Gauge (tension)
20 sts and 46 rows to 4in (10cm) over garter stitch using US 5 (3.75mm) needles.

Abbreviations
See page 17.

Pattern

Back and Fronts (made in one piece)
With US 3 (3.25mm) needles and yarn B, cast on 104(112:120) sts
Row 1 (WS): K each st tbl.
Rows 2–3: Knit.
Change to US 5 (3.75mm) needles and yarn A and cont in garter st (knit every row) until work measures 3¹/₂(4:4¹/₂)in (9(10:11)cm) from cast-on edge.
Next row: K26(28:30), turn and leave rem sts on a stitch holder.

Left back
Next row: Knit.
Next row: Cast on 2 sts, k to end.
Work garter st on these 28(30:32) sts until Left Back measures 3¹/₂(4:4¹/₂)in (9(10:11.5)cm) from point where work divides, ending at armhole edge.
Next row: K16 (18:18) and turn, leaving rem 12(12:14) sts on a holder.
Knit 3(5:7) rows.
Bind (cast) off.

Right back
Keep the center 52(56:60) sts on the holder and, with RS facing, rejoin yarn A to rem 26(28:30) sts.
Next row: Knit.
Next row: Cast on 2 sts then work Right Back to match Left Back, but reversing shaping on neck.

Front
Rejoin yarn A to sts on holder and work in garter stitch until work measures 7(8:9)in (18(20:23)cm) from cast-on edge, ending with a WS row.
Next row: K16(18:18), turn and leave rem sts on a holder.

Left front neck
Work 3(5:7) rows on these 16(18:18) sts.
Bind (cast) off.

Right front neck
Keeping center 20(20:24) sts on holder, rejoin yarn A to rem sts and work Right Front Neck to match Left Front Neck.

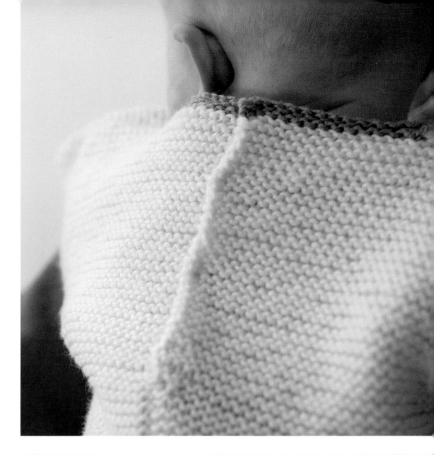

Sleeves (make two)

With US 5 (3.75mm) needles and yarn A, cast on 56(60:64) sts

Row 1 (WS): K each st tbl.

Rows 2–3: Knit.

Cont in garter st, dec 1 st at each end of 5th (WS) row then at each end of every foll 4th row 11(12:13) times. *32(34:36) sts*

Cut yarn.

Change to US 3 (3.25mm) needles and yarn B.

Knit 4 rows.

Bind (cast) off.

Neckband

Stitch shoulder seams.

Beg at opening of left back, using US 3 (3.25mm) needles and yarn B, k 12(12:14) sts from holder, pick up and k 4(6:8) sts down left of neck, pick up and k 20(20:24) sts from holder for center front, pick up and k 4(6:8) sts up right side of neck, then k 12(12:14) sts from holder for right back. *52(56:68) sts*

Next row: K11(11:13), sk2po, k1(3:5), sk2po, k16(16:20), sk2po, k1(3:5), sk2po, k11(11:13). *44(48:60) sts*

Next row: K9(9:11), sk2po, k0(2:4), sk2po, k14(14:18), sk2po, k0(2:4), sk2po, k k9(9:11). *36(40:52) sts*

Bind (cast) off.

To finish

Weave in any loose ends neatly.

Stitch sleeves in place, matching shoulder seams to center of cast-on edge of each sleeve. Stitch sleeve seams. Overlap back opening edges and stitch together at base. Stitch press fasteners, evenly spaced, on back opening.

fisherman's sweater

This rugged sweater is designed to be a favorite with outdoor types. With its textured yoke and wide neckline, it's both sturdy and stylish.

> **Knitting notes** If the prospect of following a chart is too daunting, you could work the yoke in moss stitch (see page 16) for a similar textured effect.

Yarn
3(3) 3½oz (100g) balls—approx 606(606)yds (555(555)m)—of Patons Wool Blend Aran in shade 53 Airforce

Needles
Pair each of US 6 (4.00mm) and US 7 (4.50mm) knitting needles

Extras
Tapestry needle

Sizes
2(3) years

Actual size
Chest: 27½(31in (70(78.5)cm)
Shoulder to hem: 13(13¼in (33(33.5)cm)
Sleeve seam: 8(9)in (20(22.5)cm)

Gauge (tension)
19 sts and 24 rows to 4in (10cm) over stockinette (stocking) stitch using US 7 (4.50mm) needles.

Abbreviations
See page 17.

Pattern

Back
**With US 7 (4.50mm) needles, cast on 66(74)sts sts.
Knit 4 rows.
Row 5 (WS): K4, p to last 4 sts, k4.
Row 6: Knit. Rep rows 5–6, 6 times more, then Row 5 once more.
Beg with a knit row, work in stockinette (stocking) stitch (1 row knit, 1 row purl) until work measures 8in (20.5cm) from cast-on edge, ending with a purl row.**

Yoke
Follow the chart until row 32 has been completed.

Shape neck
Patt 23(27) sts, turn and work on these sts for Right Back Neck, leaving rem sts on a holder.
Next row: Bind (cast) off 2 sts at neck edge, patt to end. *21(25) sts*
Next row: Patt to last 2 sts, k2tog. *20(24) sts*
Work 1(3) rows in patt with no further decreases.
Bind (cast) off.
Transfer center 20 sts on to holder, then work Left Back Neck to match.

Front

Work as for Back from ** to **.

Yoke

Follow the chart until row 26 has been completed.

Shape neck

Next row: Patt 26(30) sts, turn and work on these sts for Left Front Neck, leaving rem sts on a holder.

Continuing in patt, dec 1 st at neck edge on next 6 rows. *20(24) sts*

Work a further 3(5) rows in patt with no further decreases.

Bind (cast) off.

Transfer center 14 sts on to holder, then work Right Front Neck to match.

Sleeves (make two)

With US 6 (4.00mm) needles, cast on 34(38) sts.

Beg with a k row, work in stockinette (stocking) stitch for 6 rows.

Row 7: K2, [p2, k2] to end.

Row 8: P2, [k2, p2] to end.

Rep rows 7–8 once more.

Change to US 7 (4.50mm) needles and, beg with a knit row, work in stockinette (stocking) stitch, inc 1 at each end of 3rd and every foll 4th row until there are 52(60) sts.

Cont without further increases until sleeve measures 7¾(8¾)in (19.5(22)cm) from cast-on edge, ending with a knit row.

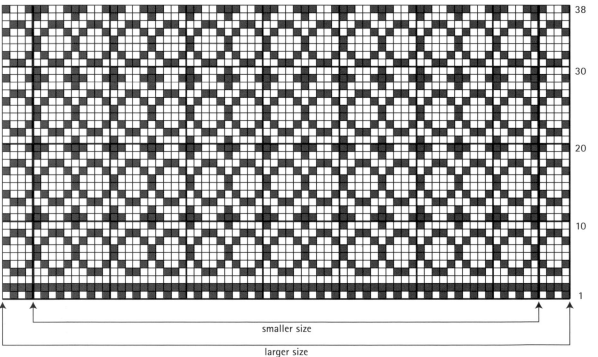

■ k on WS, p on RS

□ k on RS, p on WS

smaller size

larger size

Next row: Knit.
Rep last row twice more.
Bind (cast) off.

Neckband
Join right shoulder seam with right sides facing, oversewing cast-off edges together.
With RS facing, pick up and k 10 sts down left front neck, 14 sts from holder at center front neck, 10 sts up right front neck, 6 sts down right back neck, 20 sts from holder at center back neck, and 6 sts up left back neck. *66 sts*
Row 1: K2, [p2, k2] to end.
Row 2: P2, [k2, p2] to end.
Rep rows 1–2 once more.
Beg with a purl row, work in stockinette (stocking) stitch (1 row purl, 1 row knit) for 6 rows.
Bind (cast) off loosely knitwise.

To finish
Weave in any loose ends neatly.
Join right shoulder and neckband seam. Matching end of shoulder seam to center of cast-off edge of sleeve, attach sleeves, then join side seams from top of side slits and sleeve seams.

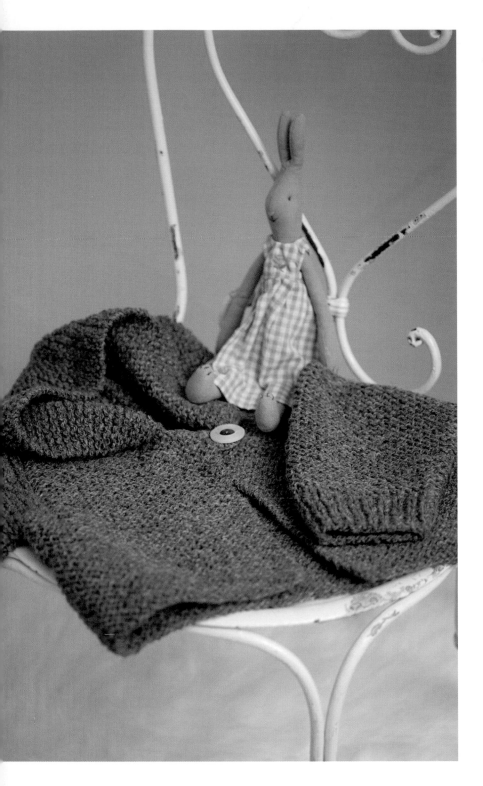

jacket with hood

Providing an extra layer of warmth, this practical, chunky jacket with a pointed hood is a winter essential for little boys and girls alike.

Yarn
4(4:5) x 3½oz (100g) balls—approx 744(744:930)yds
(680(680:850)m)—of Rowan Scottish Tweed Aran in shade
005 Lavender

Needles
Pair each of US 7 (4.50mm) and US 9 (5.50mm) knitting needles

Extras
Tapestry needle
3 stitch holders
1 x 1in (25mm) button
Sewing needle
Sewing thread to match yarn

Sizes
6(12:18) months

Actual size
Width across back: 13½(15¼:16½)in (34(38:42)cm)
Shoulder to hem: 10¾(12:13)in (27(30:33)cm)
Sleeve seam: 8(8¾:9½)in (20.5(22:24)cm)

Gauge (tension)
17 sts and 34 rows to 4in (10cm) over garter stitch using
US 9 (5.50mm) needles.

Abbreviations
See page 17.

Knitting notes The body of the jacket is made in one piece, so there are no side seams to sew up, and the simple garter stitch is quick to do and creates a lovely thick texture.

Pattern

Back and Fronts (made in one piece)

With US 9 (5.50mm) needles, cast on 108(114:120) sts. Work in garter stitch (knit every row) until work measures 5(6:6¾)in (13(15:17)cm) from cast-on edge.

Divide for armholes

Next row (WS): K25(26:28) then transfer these sts, for Right Front, to a stitch holder, bind (cast) off 7(8:8) sts, k43(45:47) and transfer these 44(46:48) sts, for Back, to another stitch holder, bind (cast) off next 7(8:8) sts, and k to end.

Left front

Cont in garter stitch on these 25(26:28) sts until work measures 8¼(9½:10½)in (21(24:27)cm) from cast-on edge, ending at the front edge.

Shape neck

Bind (cast) off 6 sts at beg of next row, 2 sts at beg of next 1(2:3) alt rows and 1st at beg of next 5(4:3) alt rows. *12(12:13) sts*

Cont in garter stitch until work measures 10½(12:13)in (27(30:33)cm) from cast-on edge.

Do not bind (cast) off but cut yarn and leave stitches on a stitch holder.

Right front

Rejoin yarn to armhole edge of sts on stitch holder and work to match Left Front, but reversing shaping.

Back

With RS facing, rejoin yarn to sts on stitch holder and cont in garter stitch until work measures 10¼(11½:12½)in (26(29:32)cm) from cast-on edge, ending with a WS row.

Shape neck

Next row (RS): K13(13:14) and transfer these sts to a stitch holder (or leave them on the needle if you prefer), bind (cast) off 18(20:20), k to end.

Next row: Working on 13(13:14) sts for Left Back, k11(11:12), k2tog. *12(12:13) sts*

Next row: Knit.

Do not bind (cast) off but cut yarn and leave stitches on a stitch holder.

Rejoin yarn to neck edge of sts for right back, k2tog, k to end. *12(12:13) sts*

Next row: Knit.

Do not bind (cast) off but cut yarn and leave stitches on a stitch holder.

Hood

With US 9 (5.50mm) needles, cast on 32(34:36) sts.

Knit 3 rows.

Next row (WS): Inc 1, k to end. *33(35:37) sts*

Cont in garter stitch, inc 1 at same edge on every foll 4th row 7 times more. *40(42:44) sts*

Cont in garter stitch without further shaping until work measures 15(15½:15¾)in (38(39:40)cm) from cast-on edge, ending with a RS row.

Next row (WS): K2tog, k to end. 39(41:43) sts

Cont in garter stitch, dec 1 at same edge on every foll 4th row 7 times more. *32(34:36) sts*

Work 3 rows in garter stitch without further shaping.

Bind (cast) off.

Sleeves (make two)

With US 7 (4.50mm) needles, cast on 39(41:43) sts.

Row 1: (RS): P1, [k1, p1] to end.

Row 2: K1, [p1, k1] to end.

Rep rows 1–2 until work measures 2in (5cm) from cast-on edge, ending with a WS row.

Change to US 9 (5.50mm) needles and, working in garter stitch, inc 1 at each end of every 8th row 4(5:5) times. *47(51:53) sts*

Cont in garter stitch without further shaping until work measures 8¾(9½:10¼)in (22(24:26)cm) from cast-on edge.

Bind (cast) off.

To finish

Weave in any loose ends neatly.

Join shoulder seams by grafting stitches from stitch holders.

Fold hood in half and join back (shaped) edges to form back seam. Fold back 1¼in (3cm) on front edge of hood and secure with a few stitches, then stitch lower edge of hood to neck edge, with front (folded) edges of hood approximately 1¼in (3cm) in from front edges of jacket (to allow jacket fronts to overlap slightly).

Join sleeve seams, starting at cuff and stopping approximately 7 rows from top. Join sleeves to armholes (match top edge of sleeve to side edges of armhole and open edge of sleeve seam to base of armhole).

Make a button loop on the right front for a girl and the left front for a boy and attach a button to the opposite side of the neck opening.

fish sweater

Knitted in a thick, soft, tweedy yarn, this is an ideal sweater for adventures in the great outdoors. The decorative band with its row of little fishes gives the sweater added appeal.

Yarn
4 x 1¾oz (50g) balls—approx 384yds (352m)—of Debbie Bliss Donegal Luxury Tweed Aran in shade 36004 red (A), 1 ball—approx 96yds (88m)—in each of shade 36006 indigo (B), and shade 36013 orange (C)

Needles
Pair each of US 8 (5.00mm) and US 7 (4.50mm) knitting needles
US 7 (4.50mm) circular needle, 16in (40cm) long

Extras
Stitch holder
Tapestry needle

Sizes
1(2:3) years

Actual size
Around chest: 26(27:28½)in (66(68.5:72.5)cm)
Back neck to hem: 13¾(14¼:14¼)in (35(36:36)cm)
Sleeve seam: 8(8¾:9½)in (20.5(22:24)cm)

Gauge (tension)
18 sts and 26 rows to 4in (10cm) over stockinette (stocking) stitch using US 8 (5.00mm) needles.

Abbreviations
See page 17.

Pattern
Back
**With US 7 (4.50mm) needles and yarn A, cast on 59(61:65) sts
Row 1: K1, [p1, k1] to end.
Row 2: P1, [k1, p1] to end.
Rep rows 1–2, 3 times more.
Change to US 8 (5.00mm) needles.
Beg with a knit row, work in stockinette (stocking) stitch (1 row knit, 1 row purl) for 15 rows, or until work measures 3½in (9cm) from cast-on edge, ending with a knit row.
Cut yarn.
Join in yarn B and purl 1 row.
Do not cut yarn B but join in yarn C and work the next 11 rows from chart, working edge stitches on 3rd size in B only.
Cut C and, with yarn B, purl 1 row.
Cut yarn.
Join in yarn A and cont in stockinette (stocking) stitch for 12 rows, or until work measures 8in (20.5cm) from cast-on edge, ending with a purl row.
Shape raglan
Bind (cast) off 2 sts at beg of next 2 rows. *55(57:61) sts*
Next row (RS): K1, skpo, k to last 3 sts, k2tog, k1.
Next row: Purl.**
Rep last 2 rows 17(18:18) times more. *19(19: 23) sts*
Bind (cast) off.

> **Knitting notes** In the same way as the Heartwarmer (see page 24), the chart for this sweater shows you the 15-stitch pattern that you need to repeat to make the band of fish. In addition the number of edge stitches needed at the begining and end of the band is marked for each size. If you are knitting the third size, work the edge stitches in yarn B only.

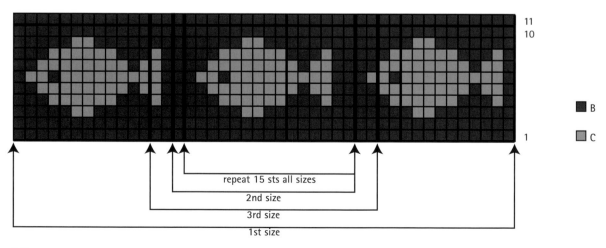

repeat 15 sts all sizes
2nd size
3rd size
1st size

■ B
□ C

Front

Work as for Back from ** to **. Rep last 2 rows 12(13:13) times more.
29(29:33) sts

Shape neck

Next row (RS): K1, skpo, k4 and turn, leaving rem sts on a holder.

Left neck

Next row: P2tog, p4. *5 sts*

Next row: K1, sk2po, k1.

Next row: P3.

Next row: K1, skpo.

Next row: P2tog and fasten off.

Right neck

With RS facing, join yarn to sts on holder, bind (cast) off 15(15:19) sts, k4, k2tog, k1.

Next row: P4, p2tog.

Next row: K1, sk2po, k1.

Next row: P3.

Next row: K2tog, k1.

Next row: P2tog and fasten off.

Sleeves (make two)

With US 7 (4.50mm) needles and yarn A, cast on 34(36:36) sts

Row 1: [K1, p1] to end.

Rep row 1, 5 times more.

Change to US 8 (5.00mm) needles.

Beg with a knit row, work in stockinette (stocking) stitch, inc 1 at each end of 3rd and every alt row until there are 42 sts, then on every foll 4th row until there are 54(58:58) sts.

Cont without further increases until sleeve measures 8(83/4:9½)in (20.5(22:24)cm) from cast-on edge, ending with a purl row.

Shape raglan

Bind (cast) off 2 sts at beg of next 2 rows. *50(54:54) sts*

Next row (RS): K1, skpo, k to last 3 sts, k2tog, k1.

Next row: Purl.

Rep last 2 rows 14(15:15) times more. *20(22:22) sts*

Left sleeve only

Dec 1 st at each end of next row.

Next row: Bind (cast) off 3 sts, p to end. *15(17:17) sts*

Next row: K1, skpo, k to end.

Next row: Bind (cast) off 4 sts, p to end.

Rep last 2 rows once more. *5(7:7) sts*

Bind (cast) off.

Right sleeve only

Next row: Bind (cast) off 4 sts, k to last 3 sts, k2tog, k1.

Next row: Purl.

Rep last 2 rows twice more. *5(7:7) sts*

Bind (cast) off.

Neckband

Join raglan seams.

With right side facing and using US 7 (4.50mm) circular needle and yarn A, omitting center stitch on front neck and starting from the next stitch to the left, pick up and knit 8(8:10) sts along right front neck, then 4 sts up right front, 15(17:17) sts from right sleeve top, 19(19:23) sts across back neck, 15(17:17) sts from left sleeve top, 4 sts down left front neck, and 8(8:10) sts across left front neck. *73(77:85) sts*

Row 1: P1, [k1, p1] to end.
Row 2: K1, [p1, k1] to end.
Rep rows 1–2, 5 times more.
Bind (cast) off in rib

To finish

Weave in any loose ends neatly.

striped jacket

A mohair yarn and subtle stripes make this little jacket look very special, yet the simple shaping and garter stitch fabric ensure that it's easy and quick to knit, even for a beginner.

Knitting notes When working in garter stitch, to create a firm, even edge to the work slip the first stitch of each row instead of knitting it. You will need only four balls of yarn, whether you make the smaller or the larger size. This is a luxury yarn so make the most of any leftovers by knitting a simple garter-stitch scarf to match the jacket.

Yarn

1 x 1³/₄oz (50g) ball—approx 153yds (140m)—of Rowan Kid Classic in each of shade 854 Tea Rose (A), shade 841 Lavender Ice (B), shade 864 Precious (C), and shade 855 Smudge (D)

Needles

Pair each of US 6 (4.00mm) and US 8 (5.00mm) knitting needles

Extras

3 stitch holders
Tapestry needle
55in (140cm) of ⁵/₈-in (15-mm) wide sheer ribbon

Sizes

1(2) years

Actual size

Width across back: 13¼(14½)in (33.5(36.5)cm)
Shoulder to hem: 11½(13)in (29(33)cm)
Sleeve seam: 8(9¼)in (20.5(23.5)cm)

Gauge (tension)

18 sts and 34 rows to 4in (10cm) over garter stitch using US 8 (5.00mm) needles.

Abbreviations

See page 17.

Pattern

Back and Fronts (made in one piece)

With US 6 (4.00mm) needles and yarn A, cast on 120(132) sts.
Row 1 (WS): K each st tbl.
Work 4(6) rows in garter stitch (knit every row).
Change to US 8 (5.00mm) needles.
Cont in garter stitch for a further 8 rows. Cut yarn.
Join in yarn B and work 14(16) rows in garter stitch. Cut yarn.
Join in yarn C and work 14(16) rows in garter stitch. Cut yarn.
Join in yarn D and work 14(16) rows in garter stitch. Cut yarn.

Divide for back and fronts

Transfer the first 30(33) sts to a stitch holder for right front. Join in yarn A, k60(66) and turn, leaving rem 30(33) sts on another holder for left front.
Working on the center 60(66) sts only, work a further 13(15) rows in garter stitch. Cut yarn.

Join in yarn B and work 14(16) rows in garter stitch. Cut yarn.

Join in yarn C and work 10(12) rows in garter stitch.

Shape back neck

Next row: K 21(23) and turn, leaving rem sts on a holder.

Work 3 rows in garter stitch for right back neck.

Bind (cast) off.

Rejoin yarn to sts on holder and bind (cast) off 18(20) sts, then k to end.

Work a further 3 rows in garter stitch.

Bind (cast) off.

Left front

Rejoin yarn A to sts on holder and work 14(16) rows in garter stitch. Cut yarn.

Join in yarn B and work 14(16) rows in garter stitch. Cut yarn.

Shape left front neck

Join in yarn C and work 7(9) rows in garter stitch, ending at front edge.

Next row: Bind (cast) off 7(8) sts, k to end.

Next row: K to last 3 sts, k2tog, k1.

Next row: K1, skpo, k to end.

Work a further 4 rows in garter stitch.

Bind (cast) off.

Right front

Work to match Left Front, but reversing shaping.

Sleeves (make two)

With US 6 (4.00mm) needles and yarn D, cast on 32(38) sts.

Row 1 (WS): K each st tbl.

Work 4(6) rows in garter stitch.

Change to US 8 (5.00mm) needles and cont in garter stitch for a further 6 rows.

Next row: Inc 1, k to last st, inc 1. *34(40) sts*

Next row: Knit.

Cut yarn.

Join in yarn A and cont in garter stitch, changing colors to B, C, and D after every 14(16) rows. At the same time, inc 1 at each end of 9th and foll 10th rows until there are 44(52) sts.

Work a further 7(8) rows in garter stitch.

Bind (cast) off.

To finish

Weave in all loose ends neatly.

Join shoulder seams. Sew top of sleeve to armhole edge, matching shoulder seam to center of cast-off edge of sleeve. Stitch sleeve seams.

Cut ribbon in half. Thread through fabric at corner of neck edge on each side, between stitches, and knot, leaving two ends of equal length on each side to tie in a decorative bow.

• porridge bear • baby blanket • colorful bunting
• sleeping robe

chapter six

bedroom accessories

porridge bear

Comfortingly soft, squashy, and huggable, this nubbly-textured teddy bear—with or without his smart red sweater and striped scarf—will make a lovely companion for any baby.

Yarn

2 x 1³/₄oz (50g) balls—approx 192yds (180m)—of Sublime Luxurious Woolly Merino in shade 175 Whiter (A)

1 x 1³/₄oz (50g) ball—approx 120yds (110m)—of Sublime Soya Cotton DK in shade 150 Sizzle (B)

1 x 1³/₄oz (50g) ball—approx 127yds (116m)—of Sublime Baby Cashmere Merino Silk DK in each of shade 03 Vanilla (C), and shade 124 Splash (D)

Small amount of 4-ply yarn in navy blue or black

Needles

Pair each of US 7 (4.50mm), US 6 (4.00mm), and US 3 (3.25mm) knitting needles

Extras

Stitch holder

Tapestry needle

Washable polyester toy filling

Size

One

Actual size

Height: 16¹/₂in (42cm)

Gauge (tension)

16 sts and 28 rows to 4in (10cm) over garter stitch using US 7 (4.50mm) needles and yarn A.

Abbreviations

See page 17.

Knitting notes Because the pattern for the bear is written row-by-row, it can easily be adapted for other yarns. Just make sure your knitted fabric is firm enough that the stuffing does not come out through the holes (you may need to use needles one or two sizes smaller than those recommended for your chosen yarn), and be prepared for your bear to be slightly taller or shorter than the one pictured here.

The bear's sweater is reversible. For older children, you may prefer to have the opening at the back and add a loop and button fastening.

Pattern

Body, head, and legs (made in one piece)
With US 7 (4.50mm) needles and yarn A, cast on 32 sts.
Knit 32 rows.
Row 33: Dec 1, k to last 2 sts, dec 1. *30 sts*
Rep row 33, 6 times more. *18 sts*
Next row: Knit.

Shape face and head
Row 1: Inc 1, k6, inc 1, k2, inc 1, k6, inc 1. *22 sts*
Row 2 and every alt row: Knit.
Row 3: Inc 1, k8, inc 1, k2, inc 1, k8, inc 1. *26 sts*
Row 5: Inc 1, k10, inc 1, k2, inc 1, k10, inc 1. *30 sts*
Row 7: Inc 1, k12, inc 1, k2, inc 1, k12, inc 1. *34 sts*
Row 9: K15, inc 1, k2, inc 1, k15. *36 sts*
Row 11: K16, inc 1, k2, inc 1, k16. *38 sts*
Row 13: K17, k2tog, k2tog tbl, k17. *36 sts*
Row 15: K16, k2tog, k2tog tbl, k16. *34 sts*
Row 17: K15, k2tog, k2tog tbl, k15. *32 sts*
Row 19: K14, k2tog, k2tog tbl, k14. *30 sts*
Row 21: K13, k2tog, k2tog tbl, k13. *28 sts*
Row 23: K12, k2tog, k2tog tbl, k12. *26 sts*
Row 24: Knit.

Shape top and back of head
Dec 1 st at each end of next and every following alt row until 18 sts rem.
Knit 1 row.
Inc 1 at each end of next and every following alt row until 26 sts rem.
Knit 15 rows without further shaping.

Shape neck
Dec 1 st at each end of next and every following alt row until 18 sts rem.
Knit 2 rows.

Shape body
Inc 1 at each end of next 7 rows. *32 sts*
Knit 32 rows without further shaping.

Divide for legs
Next row: Cast on 16 sts, turn and knit these 16 sts, then knit 16 sts from body. *32 sts*
Turn and leave rem sts on a stitch holder.
**Knit 42 rows.
Next row: [K2tog] 16 times. *16 sts*

Knit 3 rows.
Next row: [K2tog] 8 times. *8 sts*
Cut yarn and thread tail through all sts.**
Join yarn to stitches on holder, k16, cast on 16 sts, then rep from ** to ** for second leg.

Arms (make two)
With US 7 (4.50mm) needles and yarn A, cast on 14 sts.
Row 1: Inc 1, k to last st, inc 1. *16 sts*
Rep row 1, 5 times more. *26 sts*
Knit 36 rows.
Next row: [K2tog] 13 times. *13 sts*
Knit 3 rows.
Next row: K1, [k2tog] 6 times. *7 sts*
Cut yarn and thread tail of yarn through all sts.

Ears (make two)
With US 7 (4.50mm) needles and yarn A, cast on 6 sts.
Row 1: Inc 1, k to last st, inc 1. *8 sts*
Rep row 1, 3 times more. *14 sts*
Knit 4 rows.
Next row: Dec 1, k to last 2 sts, dec 1. *12 sts*
Next row: Knit.
Rep last 2 rows twice more. *8 sts*
Cut yarn and thread tail through all sts.

To finish
With black or navy yarn, embroider bear's face. Stitch the eyes and nose in satin stitch and the mouth in chain stitch.
Draw up gathering thread tightly on each leg to form feet. Right sides together, fold each leg in half and stitch inner leg seams with backstitch. Turn right side out. Stuff legs with toy filling.
Join side seams of head and body, then join body to tops of legs, leaving a small gap. Stuff with filling and close seam.
Draw up gathering thread tightly on each arm to form paws. Right sides together, fold each arm in half and stitch seams with backstitch. Turn right side out. Stuff arms with filling. Stitch arms to sides of body.
Draw up gathering thread at base of each ear, not too tightly, then stitch ears in place.

Sweater (made in one piece)

With US 3 (3.25mm) needles and yarn B, cast on 77 sts.
Row 1: K1, [p1, k1] to end.
Row 2: P1, [k1, p1] to end.
Rep rows 1–2 once more.
Change to US 6 (4.00mm) needles.
Beg with a knit row, work in stockinette (stocking) stitch (1 row knit, 1 row purl) for 4 rows.

Right front

Next row: K19, turn and leave rem sts on a stitch holder.
Next row: Purl.
Cont in stockinette (stocking) stitch on these 19 sts for a further 12 rows, ending with a purl row.

Shape front edge

Next row: Bind (cast) off 4 sts, k to end. *15 sts*
Next row: Purl.
Cont in stockinette (stocking) stitch on these 15 sts for a further 6 rows, ending with a purl row.

Shape neck

Next row: Bind (cast) off 6 sts, k to end. *9 sts*
Next row: Purl.
Work a further 2 rows in stockinette (stocking) stitch, ending with a purl row.

Shape shoulder

Next row: K6, turn.
Next row: Sl1, p5.
Next row: K3, turn.
Next row: Sl1, p2.
Next row: K9.
Next row: Bind (cast) off all sts purlwise. Cut yarn.
Keeping center 39 sts on a stitch holder for Back, rejoin yarn to rem 19 sts and work Left Front to match Right Front, but reversing shaping.

Back

Rejoin yarn to 39 sts on holder and, beg with a knit row, work 20 rows in stockinette (stocking) stitch.

Shape right back neck

Next row: K13 sts and leave rem sts on a holder.
Cont in stockinette (stocking) stitch, dec 1 st at neck edge on next 4 rows, ending with a knit row. *9 sts*
Work a further 2 rows in stockinette (stocking stitch), ending with a knit row.

Shape shoulder

Next row: P6, turn.
Next row: Sl1, k5.
Next row: P3, turn.
Next row: Sl1, k2.
Next row: P9.
Next row: Bind (cast) off all sts.

Keeping center 13 sts on holder, rejoin yarn to rem 13 sts and work left side of Back to match right side, but reversing shaping.

Armhole bands

With US 3 (3.25mm) needles and yarn B, with right side of work facing, pick up and knit 43 sts around each armhole.
Row 1: P1, [k1, p1] 21 times.
Row 2: K1, [p1, k1] 21 times.
Next row: As row 1.
Bind (cast) off in rib.
Stitch shoulder seams.

Neckband

On Right Front, with right side facing, pick up and knit 9 sts up front edge.
Row 1: P1, [k1, p1] 4 times.
Row 2: K1, [p1, k1] 4 times.
Next row: As row 1.
Bind (cast) off in rib.
On Left Front, with right side facing, pick up and knit 9 sts down front edge.
Row 1: K1, [p1, k1] 4 times.
Row 2: P1, [k1, p1] 4 times.
Next row: As row 1.
Bind (cast) off in rib.
Beg at top of right front band, pick up and knit 13 sts on right front neck, 13 sts down right back neck, 13 sts from holder, 13 sts up left back neck and 13 sts along right front neck. *65 sts*
Row 1: P1, [k1, p1] 32 times.
Row 2: K1, [p1, k1] 32 times.
Next row: As row 1.
Bind (cast) off in rib.

To finish

Weave in any loose ends neatly. Join front seam.

Scarf

With US 7 (4.50mm) needles and yarn C, cast on 12 sts.
Knit 2 rows.
Do not cut yarn, but join in yarn D.
Knit 2 rows in D.
Knit 2 rows in C.
Rep last 4 rows 61 times more, or until work measures 22¾in (58cm) from cast-on edge, ending with 2 rows in C.
Bind (cast) off using yarn C.

To finish

Weave in any loose ends neatly.

baby blanket

A cellular blanket is the classic choice to keep your baby warm. A square shape allows the blanket to be folded in half diagonally for swaddling, or opened out to use as a cot cover.

Knitting notes Though this blanket is worked in rows, it is advisable to work back and forth on a circular knitting needle as this accommodates a greater number of stitches than a pair of straight needles and helps to distribute the weight of the knitting more evenly.

Yarn
8 x 1¾oz (50g) balls—approx 1136yds (1040m)—of Rowan Cashsoft Baby DK, in shade 800 Snowman

Needles
US 6 (4.00mm) circular knitting needle, from 16–40in (40–100cm) long

Extras
Tapestry needle

Size
One

Actual size
33½ x 33½in (85 x 85cm)
Border: 2in (5cm) wide

Gauge (tension)
17 sts and 36 rows to 4in (10cm) over seed (moss) stitch, using US 6 (4.00mm) needles.

Abbreviations
See page 17.

Pattern

Blanket (made in one piece)
With US 6 (4.00mm) needle, cast on 145 sts.
Row 1: Sl1 knitwise, [p1, k1] to end.
Rep row 1 until work measures 2in (5cm) from cast-on edge.

Begin cellular patt
Row 1: Sl1 knitwise, [p1, k1] 5 times, k1, [yo, k2tog] 61 times, k1, [p1, k1] 5 times.
Row 2: Sl1 knitwise, [p1, k1] 5 times, k124 (or to last 10 sts), [p1, k1] 5 times.
Row 3: As row 2 Rows 1–3 form patt, rep until work measures 31½in (80cm) from cast-on edge, ending with row 2 of patt.
Next row: Sl1 knitwise, [p1, k1] to end.
Rep last row until work measures 33½in (85cm) from cast-on edge.
Bind (cast) off knitwise.

To finish
Weave in any loose ends neatly.

colorful bunting

Don't save this bunting for a special occasion: festive flags make a cheerful decoration for the nursery or play room and can be strung across the ceiling or along a shelf edge. They are also suitable for outdoor use.

Yarn
1 x 1¾oz (50g) ball—approx 92yds (84m)—of Debbie Bliss Cotton DK in each of shade 01 white, shade 47 red, shade 44 pink, shade 53 blue, shade 54 emerald green, shade 55 grass green, and shade 56 buttermilk

Needles
US 6 (4.00mm) circular needle, 40in (100cm) long

Extras
Tapestry needle

Actual size
Single pennant: 3¼in (8cm) long by 3¼in (8cm) wide
Total length of bunting: approx 3½yds (3.25m)

Gauge (tension)
It is not necessary to achieve a specific gauge for this project, but these flags are approximately 20 sts to 4in (10cm) over garter stitch using US 6 (4mm) needles.

Abbreviations
See page 17.

Pattern

With US 6 (4.00mm) needles and white yarn, cast on 620 sts.
Bind (cast) off.
Count 90 sts from end of bound (cast) off row.
*With US 6 (4.00mm) needles and yarn in colour of your choice, pick up and k next 15 sts.

Make pennant

Row 1: Sl1, k to end.
Row 2: As row 1.
Row 3: K1, skpo, k to last 3 sts, k2tog, k1.
Row 4: As row 1.
Rep rows 1-4, 4 times more. *5 sts*
Next row: Sl1, k to end.
Next row: K1, sk2po, k1. *3 sts*
Next row: Sl1, k2.
Next row: Sl1, k2.
Next row: Sk2po.
Fasten off.
Leave next 10 sts of cast-off (bound-off) edge unworked and rejoin yarn to next st.*
Rep from * to * until you have made 18 pennants (3 in each color).

To finish

Weave in ends as neatly as possible.

> **Knitting notes** This pattern produces a 3½yds (3.25m) length of bunting with 18 flags; there is approximately 18in (46cm) free of flags at either end, for tying. For a longer length, add an extra 25 sts to the cast-on row for each additional flag; alternatively, for a shorter length, reduce the cast-on row by 25 sts for each flag. Any pure cotton double-knitting weight yarn can be used for this project, in the colors of your choice to match nursery decor or to create a party mood.

sleeping robe

This all-in-one will keep your baby as snug as can be. Buttons at the shoulders make it simple to get on and off and a drawstring hem creates a cozy cocoon, as well as making nappy changing quick and easy.

Knitting notes The main part of this garment is a tube, simply and quickly knitted in the round on a circular needle. After casting on, work the first few rows of the pattern back and forth, as if you were using a pair of knitting needles, to avoid the work becoming twisted, then begin knitting in the round to create a seamless tube of fabric. Sew up the tiny bit of open seam once the knitting is completed.

When it comes to the yoke, sleeves, and neckbands, you can use the same circular needle, working back and forth in rows, or you can swap to straight needles if you prefer.

Yarn
5(6) x 1³/₄oz (50g) balls—approx 470(564)yds (344(430)m)—of Sublime Cashmere Merino Silk Aran in shade 0168 Polo
Scraps of similar weight yarn for embroidery

Needles
US 6 (4.00mm) circular knitting needle, 16in (40cm) long
US 7 (4.50mm) circular knitting needle, 16in (40cm) long
2 US 6 (4.00mm) double-pointed knitting needles

Extras
Tapestry needle
8 x ¹/₂in (12mm) buttons
Sewing needle
Sewing thread to match yarn

Sizes
0-3(3-6) months

Actual size
Around chest: 19¹/₂(22¹/₄)in (49.5(56.5)cm)
Shoulder to hem: 23¹/₂(26)in (59.5(66)cm)
Sleeve seam: 7(8)in (18(20.5)cm)

Gauge (tension)
18 sts and 24 rows to 4in (10cm) over stockinette (stocking) stitch using US 7 (4.50mm) needles.

Abbreviations
See page 17.

Pattern

Back
With US 6 (4.00mm) needle, cast on 88(100) sts.
Round 1: [K1, p1] to end.
Round 2: As round 1.
Round 3 (eyelets): K1, *yo, k2tog, p1, k1, rep from * to last 3 sts, yo, k2tog, p1.
Rounds 4–6: As round 1.
Change to US 7 (4.50mm) needle and work in stockinette (stocking) stitch (every round knit) until work measures 17³/₄(19)in (45(48)cm) from cast-on edge.

Back raglan shaping
**Next row: Bind (cast) off 2 sts, k41(47) sts, turn and leave rem sts on holder.
Next row: Bind (cast) off 2 sts, p to end. Next row: K1, skpo, k to last 3 sts, k2tog, k1.
Next row: Purl.**
Rep last 2 rows 10(14) times more. *18(16) sts*
Bind (cast) off.

Front

Rejoin yarn to sts on holder and work as for Back from ** to **.

Rep last 2 rows 7(11) times more. *24(22) sts*

Left neck

Next row: K1, skpo, k4, turn and leave rem sts on a holder.

Next row: Dec 1, p to end.

Next row: K1, skpo, k2.

Next row: Dec 1, p to end.

Next row: K1, skpo.

Next row: P2 tog.

Fasten off.

Right neck

Rejoin yarn to sts on holder and bind (cast) off 10(8) sts, then work Right Neck to match Left Neck, but reversing shaping.

Sleeves (make two)

With US 6 (4.00mm) needle, cast on 33(35) sts.

Round 1: K1, [p1, k1] to end.

Round 2: P1, [k1, p1] to end.

Rep rows 1–2 twice more.

Change to US 7 (4.50mm) needle and work in stockinette (stocking) stitch, inc 1 at each end of 5th then on every foll 8th row 4(6) times. *43(49)sts*

Cont in stockinette (stocking) stitch (1 row knit, 1 row purl) until work measures 7(8)in (18(20.5)cm) from cast-on edge, ending with a purl row.

Raglan shaping

Next row (RS): Bind (cast) off 2 sts, k to end.

Next row: Bind (cast) off 2 sts, p to end.

Next row: K1, skpo, k to last 3 sts, k2tog, k1.

Next row: Purl. Rep last 2 rows until 17(15) sts rem, ending with a knit row.

Shape top

Left sleeve only

Next row: Bind (cast) off 8 sts, p to end. *9(7) sts*

Next row: K1, skpo, k to end.

Next row: Bind (cast) off purlwise.

Right sleeve only

Next row: Purl.

Next row: Bind (cast) off 8 sts, k to last 3 sts, k2tog, k1.

Next row: Bind (cast) off purlwise.

Cord tie

With US 6 (4.00mm) double-pointed needles, cast on 3 sts.

Row 1: K3, do not turn but slide sts to other end of needle.

Rep row 1, pulling yarn tightly across back of work, until work measures 35½(37¾)in (90(96)cm).

Bind (cast) off.

Back neckband

Join back raglan seams.

With RS facing and using US 6 (4.00mm) needle, pick up and k 16 sts across top of right sleeve, 15 sts across back neck, and 16 sts across top of left sleeve.
47 sts

Row 1: P1, [k1, p1] to end.

Row 2: K1, [p1, k1] to end.

Rep rows 1–2 once more.

Bind (cast) off in rib.

Front neckband

With RS facing and using US 6 (4.00mm) needle, pick up and k 21 sts across front neck.

Row 1: P1, [k1, p1] to end.

Row 2: K1, [p1, k1] to end. Rep rows 1–2 once more.

Bind (cast) off in rib.

Button bands

Starting at base of raglan, stitch the first ³⁄₄in (2cm) of the seam on each side.

With RS facing and using US 6 (4.00mm) needle, pick up and k 23(25) sts along raglan edge of left sleeve.

Row 1: P1, [k1, p1] to end.

Row 2: K1, [p1, k1] to end.

Rep rows 1–2 once more.

Bind (cast) off in rib.

Rep for right sleeve.

Front buttonhole bands

With RS facing and using US 6 (4.00mm) needle, pick up and k 24(26) sts along raglan edge of right front.

Row 1: [K1, p1] to end.

Row 2 (buttonholes): K1, *[p1, k1] twice, yo, k2tog, rep from * 3 times more, p1, [k1, p1] once (twice).

Work 2 more rows in rib, then bind (cast) off in rib.

Rep on left side.

To finish

Weave in any loose ends neatly.

Using lazy daisy and satin stitch (see page 21), embroider simple flowers, using photograph as guide for position.

Stitch buttons to button bands to correspond with buttonholes, four on each side. Thread cord through eyelets in hem.

index

suppliers

US
Debbie Bliss yarns
Sirdar yarns
Knitting Fever Inc.
P.O. Box 502
Roosevelt
New York 11575
Tel: (516) 546 3600
www.knittingfever.com

Rowan yarns
Coats Patons yarns
Westminster Fibers Inc.
4 Townsend West
Suite 8
Nashua NH 03063
Tel: 603 886 5041
www.westminsterfibers.com

CANADA
Debbie Bliss yarns
Coats Patons yarns
Rowan yarns
Sirdar yarns
Diamond Yarns Ltd
155 Martin Ross Avenue
Unit 3
Toronto
Ontario M3J 2L9
Tel: 001 416 736 6111
www.diamondyarn.com

UK
Debbie Bliss yarns
Designer Yarns Ltd
Units 8-10 Newbridge
Industrial Estate
Pitt Street
Keighley
West Yorkshire, BD21 4PQ
Tel: 01535 664222
www.designeryarns.uk.com

Rowan yarns
Coats Patons yarns
Coats/Rowan
Green Lane Mill
Holmfirth
West Yorkshire HD9 2DX
Tel: 01484 681881
www.knitrowan.com

Sirdar yarns
Sirdar Spinning Ltd
Flanshaw Lane
Wakefield
West Yorkshire
WF2 9ND
Tel: 01924 371501
www.sirdar.co.uk